How Did I Get Here?

How Did I Get Here?

To Fiona

Hope it brings back
some memories of your own.

Gordon

A MEMOIR | VOLUME 1

Rebel Without a Clue!

GORDON CRAIGIE

First published in Scotland in 2020 by
iScot Media, PO Box 26683
Helensburgh, G84 4EB

ISBN: 978-1-8382500-2-7
ebook ISBN: 978-1-8382500-3-4

Edited by Angela Valente *www.aveditorial.com*
Typeset by Laura Kincaid *www.tenthousand.co.uk*
Cover design by Thom Burgess *www.captchastudios.co.uk*
Cover image by Ian Bain

Printed by Bell & Bain Ltd, Glasgow

This book is dedicated to four very special people:

To my late mother, father and brother:
Ellen (Ella) Cooper Craigie, née McIntosh, 1922–1999
Thomas (Tom) Crawford Craigie, 1926–2011
Thomas (Tommy) Craigie, 1946–1989
without whom this book would not have been possible,
and for making my journey to adulthood everything
that I could have wished for.

And to Angela Valente, my wife and soulmate, without
whose constant encouragement and belief this book would
never have been written, and for making me complete.

———

Grateful thanks to Ken McDonald for inviting me into
the iScot family and for his support and encouragement,
allowing me to be myself as a writer.

Contents

Introduction

I never set out to write a funny book but, apparently, it is! However, you, as the reader, will be best placed to judge that...

I explain in the prologue, which follows this, how exactly this book came about, but I think the genesis of the project is probably best summed up by lyrics from the Talking Heads' song "Once in a Lifetime":

> *And you may find yourself in a beautiful house*
> *With a beautiful wife*
> *And you may ask yourself, well*
> *How did I get here?*

Given the accuracy of the first two lines, that's exactly how I feel sometimes and, hopefully, writing this book has helped me to answer that question in my own mind.

PROLOGUE

In my life

(2012)

There are places I remember
All my life, though some have changed
Some forever not for better
Some have gone and some remain…

Here's the thing, the idea for this book came to me while I was running through an unfamiliar bit of my home town, Dundee. I'm not saying this is a good thing or a bad thing, just a thing. You see, I say unfamiliar, yet I lived there for pretty much a whole year when I was nine years old, and that's a long time when you're nine. Yet still, unfamiliar. And, as my mind wandered while I ran, I thought about the other places I'd lived and how strange it is that you never, or hardly ever, set foot in those buildings again after you move.

House number one has been modernised and extended to an almost unrecognisable extent, while number two still looks largely the same, from the outside. It's in this unfamiliar part of town… Number three looms large in my mind, for reasons which will become obvious as we progress, while number four, the first house I ever bought myself, has also been extensively changed. Funnily enough, that one never really enters my mind. At least, not my conscious mind, but I do have occasional dreams where we're moving back there... no idea what that means.

Back to the run. As my mind ricocheted off in another direction, I realised that each of my three schools has been demolished, as has my teacher training college, and my university is now largely unrecognisable too. Good job I did my postgraduate degree online – at least the internet is safe from demolition! Or is it? Cyberterrorism?

Anyway, I digress, but almost certainly not for the last time. No, the point is... well, there are many points really. For instance, as we proceed on our life journey, we view everything – past, present and future – through changing lenses. That's what I mean about the unfamiliar familiar streets – they just look so different through my current lens than they did through my nine-years-old version. Many of these memories are, as I write this, foggy through grief, as we've both, my wife and I, experienced life-changing bereavements in the past year.

What worries me in particular is that just as these memories inevitably become misty in the rear-view mirror I have only now just realised explicitly that the physical memories are disappearing too. My story is disappearing without trace yet, when I close my eyes, I can see snapshots of the houses I grew up in and the schools I attended, and these images trigger other memories of people and places and events and, well, everything really. I suppose that's what is driving this exercise, that I should revisit everything and get these mental images recorded now before they too are forgotten. Wish my dad had done that...

I always thought I'd start a book with a prologue. That idea has fascinated me from the days of Frankie Howerd in *Up Pompeii*. Yet, in a novel twist on the "policemen getting younger" scenario, when I recently mentioned said Frankie to my twenty-something hairdresser – why his name came up escapes me but it must've been related to the prologue in some way! – she looked completely blank and simply said, "Who's Frankie Howerd?" Ouch! Another digression, and so soon…

The point this time is that I'm committing to this prologue before writing the book. You may think that's the way all prologues are written, but I think not. Most people write the introduction *after* they've finished. So, at this stage, this is what I think I'm going to be writing about. But if you're browsing this in a bookshop before deciding to purchase (do – I really think you'll enjoy it!) then you may be best advised to skip on two hundred pages to the epilogue, which I'll have written after I've finished and will actually confirm what I've actually written about. But still buy it… please?

So, what am I writing? Memoir? Autobiography? Sort of… but anyone who knows me will think that very odd since I have the reputation of aspiring to an ex-directory address and have frequently, but incorrectly, been referred to as Secret Squirrel. These are gross exaggerations, of course. The Secret Squirrel thing was started by an old friend when he couldn't figure out whether I was at home or meandering around Scotland, as I was prone to do at the time. I think he thought I should check in with him before I set off anywhere, which was clearly never going to happen. Of course, this description was seized on by my dad, who thought it was hilarious and proceeded to use it for the next 20-odd years! The truth is simply that I don't believe in giving too much information away unnecessarily. It's my business and I'll decide when and to whom I divulge particular details or snippets.

So, if that seems slightly at odds with attempting to write a sort of memoir or autobiography, then what exactly am I aiming for? Well, it's probably a bit like John and Paul described in "In My Life" – it's about places, people and events. It's actually more about recollections, with no desire to embarrass anyone, least of all myself, with controversial revelations. I'm not even sure I've got any of that in my locker anyway, but if I do, you ain't gonna read it here! I'm not a celebrity, and all of my achievements, so far, are relatively normal and low-key.

Note the lack of certainty there though – "so far"… No, I think what I'm doing is inviting you on a journey. It may be my journey, but I hope you recognise places, people and events from your own past and maybe, just maybe, it'll stir something in you. It may turn out to be a story of our times, those of us who straddle the cusp of baby boomers and Generation X. Or, it may not…

CHAPTER 1

In the beginning

(1959–1964)

This tale kicks off around July 1958. Never mind misty in the rear-view mirror, all of what follows in these opening paragraphs is pretty much based on anecdote and speculation. Not the best sell for a story, granted, but it's the best we've got given that all of the main actors are sadly no longer with us.

So, what apparently happened in that summer of '58 was that Mum and Dad – Ella and Tom – bundled my brother, Tommy, and, presumably, a couple of suitcases into a car borrowed from my paternal grandfather, who I was only ever to meet once, but that's a story for later. Their destination was Thurso for a holiday visit to Dad's younger brother, my Uncle Andy, who was working at the Dounreay atomic energy "thingmy" at the time. Not a journey to be undertaken by the faint-hearted, it must be said, particularly at that time. Anyway, a good time must have been had by all, with Mum and Dad creating their own brand of nuclear fusion, resulting in my arrival nine months later. Afterthought or happy surprise? Who knows, but I duly made my way onto the scene fully 13 years after my brother to complete our nuclear, almost literally, family.

Before we get fully into our stride, maybe this is the time to fill in some background information, just so we're all clear on who's who and what's what. You've already "met" Mum, Dad and Tommy, but what about their back stories?

Ella and Tom met, like most couples of their generation, at the dancing around April 1942. Twenty-one-year-old Ella lived in a tenement in Dallfield Walk, just off the Hilltown in Dundee, with her parents, Liz and Harry, and her siblings, Henry, Bette and Nan. Tom, at just 16 (!), was the oldest of six children, and lived upstairs with his grannie, while his mum, Agnes, looked after Rose, Andy, Patsy, Jimmy and Margaret downstairs in their Brook Street tenement. His dad, Andrew, was abroad in the army, but clearly visited home regularly enough!

As another teaser for much later in this saga, although Dad would only very rarely mention his father, any time he did he would only ever refer to him as Frosty Face.

Anyway, during their courtship, young Tom was learning his trade as an electrician while Ella worked in Keiller's sweetie factory, a Dundee institution, before being conscripted into the Land Army – electrician was a reserved occupation so, thankfully, Tom was not called up for military duties. Well, not then anyway.

They got engaged in 1944, married in 1945 and Tommy arrived in 1946 – and yes, the dates all work out!

By the time Tommy entered the post-war world, Tom's luck on the military front had run out and he was collared for national service. The stories he used to tell about this fascinated me – it seemed like he spent all his time playing football or otherwise enjoying himself with activities which were... well, let's just say, not as described in the army brochures!

For example, when he was stationed in Germany one of his jobs was to drive around and pick up any tyres that other army vehicles had abandoned at the side of the road. This naturally brought him into contact with many of the locals, and once he and his mates had found out that coffee was a tradeable commodity, that afforded him the opportunity to do a wee bit of wheeling and dealing. This scam earned the prototype Del-Boys enough to buy, outright, a brand-new Volkswagen Beetle straight off the assembly line, which they then used to visit anywhere and everywhere that took their fancy during their downtime. Aye, it's all fun and games until...

Despite having no choice in the matter, when guys of that generation were called up for their national service there was no obligation for either their employer to keep their job open for them or for the government to arrange an alternative. So, on returning to civvie street, Tom was jobless and now had a family to support.

Although he was a fully qualified sparkie, apart from the odd temporary job, he ended up taking anything he could find, including a spell as a tram driver, before finally securing a position in the stores of an electrical wholesaler where his knowledge of the trade would prove invaluable. So much so that this would prove to be his career path and he would stay with the same company, Wood and Cairns, progressing through Branch Manager to Scottish Director, until he left over 30 years later to start his own business.

That's actually the first time I've ever thought the whole thing through and... wow! Anyway, that's a wee blast through the family background and we can now return to... April 1959.

Back in those days, before ultrasound scans or crystal-swinging hokum-pokum, somehow or other Mum and Dad were convinced that the impending new arrival was of the female persuasion, and they were therefore looking forward to welcoming *Alison* into the world. Hopefully they weren't too disappointed when they saw little old me.

Dad certainly wasn't as, allegedly, when he visited Mum in Dundee Royal Infirmary after his work, not knowing I had arrived, he walked right by me and asked her how she was doing. When she indicated the bundle between her and the next bed, he said something along the lines of, "That's a braw-looking bairn – whose is it?"

Not that I remember any of this – I was very young at the time! Anyway, without any surgical intervention Alison was quickly changed to Gordon, apparently because Mum's older brother Henry had been in the Gordon Highlanders. He was killed in World War II and, as he had been the last male in her line, I was also given the middle name McIntosh in order to keep it going. And so, although they went into this eagerly anticipating an Alison, it was wee Gordon McIntosh Craigie whom they proudly took home…

And that home was to be 65 Ireland Street in Carnoustie, a small town on the east coast of Scotland, famous mainly for its magnificent golf courses. Far superior to St Andrews, in my humble opinion, but somehow relegated by the weight of history, Tom Morris, the R&A and all that stuff.

Carnoustie was developing as a commuter town, mainly for my birthplace, Dundee, and hovered around the 3,000-inhabitants mark in my early years. It was a great place to grow up in. Safe, despite my best efforts, and thriving. Especially in summer when the population pretty much doubled with, mainly, Glaswegian holidaymakers. Everything started to change in the 1970s though when the Weegies discovered Mallorca, and traditional Scottish seaside holiday destinations like Carnoustie and Arbroath were started on a slow but steady decline.

We lived around 100 yards from Newton Panbride Church of Scotland and it was there, on 17 May 1959, that I was duly "baptised in the name of the Father and of the Son and of the Holy Spirit and brought into the Fellowship of the Church". Not an occasion I remember of course, being very young at the time (I know I've used that one before, but it's still funny, no?), but perhaps the whole process of having water chucked at me and being called names (another old joke, but another good one!) contributed to my subsequent non-attendance and also my current, and long-established, religious stance of playing very much on the atheistic wing of the agnostic persuasion!

I don't remember too much prior to going to school, just one or two hazy memories of things happening in the house. One of those memories is of my pedal car being sold and a man coming round to our house to see it. It seems ridiculous now to think of how I could've manoeuvred that thing around our not-overly-spacious house – I must've had incredible driving skills for one so young. Either that or our furniture must've exhibited many signs of vehicle fatigue.

I can also remember playing cards with Mum, a technique she used to ensure I could recognise numbers and count before I went to school. She also, allegedly, taught me to read the local newspaper before I went to school, though whether that's a testament to my innate abilities or a comment on the standard of *The Courier* journalism is open to debate. Either way, what a great start in life. Thanks, Mum.

Our home was a modest, two-bedroomed semi-detached bungalow separated from the main east coast railway line by a none-too-sturdy hedge. We got used to it and never really noticed the trains passing, but visitors used to jump out of their skins when an express to or from Aberdeen went hurtling by. Cutting the hedge was an interesting task for Dad too, especially the other side, which involved dangling precipitously over the aforementioned railway! Anyway, Mum and Dad had the front bedroom, facing the railway, and I shared the back bedroom, indeed a bed, with my brother until I was eight years old – he left when he got married in 1967. Having an older brother was great, but a bit strange, and my early memories of Tommy centre almost exclusively around football, the Beatles and winklepickers...

The football bit is easy to explain. I firmly believe that football is in the blood. Back in the 1920s, Dad's Uncle Willie had dragged him along to Tannadice every fortnight, thus ensuring that each ensuing generation would have Dundee United-coloured blood flowing through their veins. I say Dundee United-coloured as the actual colour would vary over the years. When said Willie started off, his blood would've been green and white (from Dundee Hibernian) but metamorphosed to the black and white of Dundee United before Dad came on the scene. Hence, like both him and my brother before me, I entered this world with that black-and-white stuff providing my life source. Yet, just like Willie, we all eventually metamorphosed too and acquired the tangerine and black variety in 1969 when our club decided to modernise itself. There may well be a few more mentions of the World-Famous Dundee United FC as our story progresses...

I suppose the Beatles and winklepickers are closely related, but in my mind they're entirely separate. I don't even really remember the winklepickers per se, but I do remember Dad telling the tale on so many occasions.

Apparently, and everyone will have their own analogous version of this, Tommy pestered our parents relentlessly for a pair of winklepickers. For the uninitiated, winklepickers were the pointed-toe shoes made popular by the Beatles and others around the time teenagers were first invented, in the early 1960s. Wisely, our parents told him they would hurt his feet, they looked ridiculous, were a waste of money and no, he wasn't getting a pair. Constant badgering and, no doubt, many teenage strops later, they relented, as parents normally do, and Tommy became the proud owner of a shiny new pair of winklepickers.

The big night came, probably a Friday, and the new acquisitions were christened as he headed out to either the YMCA or Swanny's café with visions of exuding the ultimate cool and drawing admiring glances from his friends and female admirers. Whether that is what actually happened or not is lost in the mists of time, but what we do know is that he arrived home crippled, hurled the winklepickers into a corner from which they would never emerge again, and muttered, "Sorry Dad, you were right!" Ach well...

Tommy had the Beatles' first two albums, *Please, Please Me* and *With the Beatles*, all the early singles and EPs, and must've been a member of the official fan club as I also recall a few of those floppy, thin plastic, 45-rpm discs that were given away to fans at Christmas.

I vividly remember sitting in our bedroom looking at Tommy's record player and wondering how those four guys managed to get inside that sliver of vinyl! To this day I still cannot figure out how records, tapes, CDs and MP3s actually work. I know the theory, I can recite chapter and verse about electrical impulses and digital codes with the best of them, but I still don't get it. But I do remember listening to those records and being familiar with their faces and appearance, and the whole thing fascinates me still. Thanks, Tom.

Mind you, it's just as well that young Tommy had some musical taste as the only other things on offer in our house were The Alexander Brothers, Engelbert Humperdinck, Ken Dodd, Tom Jones, Lena Martell, Val Doonican and Mantovani – my record collection could've ended up entirely different!

Dad was always singing though. Sometimes they were old Scots things like "The Muckin' o' Geordie's Byre" and "An Auld Maid in the Garret", sometimes nonsense things like "Maresiedoats" and "Little Sir Echo", or sentimental stuff like "I Saw Mummy Kissing Santa Claus", but mainly what we now know as crooner tunes – things by Dean Martin, Nat King Cole, Frank Sinatra, etc. He was a good singer, even though I'm biased, and he showed no qualms about getting up in public to belt something out. At family events he would often duet with his youngest brother, Jimmy, which always came as a surprise as neither of them normally sought the limelight.

Before car radios were the norm, I suppose he was our in-car entertainment system. He was good at multitasking, mind, as he was also the satnav and tour guide. Mum used to keep telling him to keep his eyes on the road as he was always scanning the surrounding area for places of interest. Mind you, he used to frequently steer with his knees so I suppose his entire approach to driving was not exactly textbook! Still, that ability kept him at the wheel until he was 84, and he never had an accident. (He also passed that knee-steering thing on to his younger son, a skill (?) that still terrifies my wife on a regular basis!)

In my conscious lifetime, we always had a car, though that was not the case when I was born or immediately prior to that life-changing event. The reason my parents had to borrow a car for the Thurso escapade was because Dad had to sell his car, his first car, his pride and joy, to raise the £50 they were short of for buying the house in Carnoustie. £50? Even allowing for inflation and changing values, it's still hard to comprehend that £50 was almost a deal-breaker on a house purchase.

Anyway, car sold, house bought, baby on the way and the family had escaped the immediate environs of the previous generations. They were pioneers. First in either family to buy a house. First in either family to leave Dundee. Staggering stuff.

There was probably a lot of anguish at the prospect of them moving away and that things would never be the same again. I wonder if anyone had noticed that Carnoustie was only 12 miles away, 10 minutes by train and 30 minutes by bus? So close in fact that my now carless dad used to get the train to Dundee each day to go to work, taking my brother with him for his last year of primary school. He even got the train home and back at lunchtime! Simpler times.

In fact, Dad always came home for his lunch. I say lunch but, being Scottish, at the time we called it dinner or, to be strictly accurate, in oor hoose, "denner". With hindsight, this was probably the reason that he worked late every night. Mum always used to complain that he was "polishing the bins", her way of saying he did too much, but whatever he was doing he was seldom home before 8 p.m. and it was frequently after 10 p.m.

For my first couple of years at school he used to drop me off, probably in the red Austin A40 that I can just about remember. Later that became a sky-blue Austin 1100, registration AGS 669B. He used to tell a funny story about having difficulty getting into that car when he was in Perth on business one day. Whatever way he turned the key he wasn't getting in. After a while this attracted the attention of a parking attendant and, as the clearly intrigued attendant approached, Dad happened to glance to his side, only to see an identical sky-blue Austin 1100 further down the car park. Only that one had a football on the back shelf – my football! He sheepishly acknowledged he'd been trying to get into the wrong car and made good his escape while the attendant tried to figure out if he was for real or not!

While we're on the subject of cars, I might as well run through the entire timeline – as Magnus Magnusson famously always said, "I've started, so I'll finish." Next up then, there would be a brilliant white Vauxhall Victor (GTS 999F) notable for having a solid bench front seat and a revolutionary steering-wheel-mounted gearshift. And red vinyl – lots of red vinyl.

Then followed the first of Dad's bright red Ford Cortinas (OYJ 836K). This one I remember vividly as I was involved in the selection process. We had all the brochures and colour charts, and despite my best efforts to persuade him towards a Ford Capri – yes we're talking early '70s here – the Cortina won out in the end. The first day he came home with that car coincided with a parents' night at my school and I still remember the feelings of excitement turning up in this shiny, brand-new car with my dad.

The second Cortina (P-something – used to know the reg! – same colour) was an estate car as, by this time, he'd decided it would be more useful for "carrying stuff in". Whatever "stuff" was, this was obviously important to him as the third in the red Cortina trilogy, FLS 452V, was also an estate. That was the first one I was to drive, and it was made to last for many years until, eventually, he downsized to a burgundy VW Polo.

That one also hung around for way too many years until we surprised him one Christmas by gifting him our old red BMW 316i, specially valeted and polished up for the occasion. We put a red ribbon and bow across the windscreen, then led him to the car blindfolded – when we did the big reveal, his face was a picture! Not as much of a picture as ours when, as he was driving us round to Christmas dinner at my in-laws' house, the car was behaving very strangely indeed. It was like we had introduced some kangaroo-type element to the fuel system as the car shuddered its way round.

So worrying was this that I decided to drive it round the block to see if I could work out what was wrong. It's not a great feeling when you've just given your dad a car, one that's driven perfectly well in the six or so years you've had it, that you've just had serviced, MOTd and valeted, and then it drives like a tank about to expire. But... perfect! It drove exactly as it had when we'd brought it down the road a couple of hours earlier. Spooky.

Anyway, I get Dad back in the car to let him know everything's OK, but as soon as he takes off, it's kangaroo time again. I can't figure this out, and he's getting annoyed with me asking him questions, and I'm getting annoyed with him for getting annoyed with me, and... well, Christmas Day is not getting off to the best of starts. So we swap seats and off we go again with me back in control and everything is as it should be.

I tell him it must be him and we have another exchange of annoyances before exchanging seats again and returning to our kangaroo court. Despite his obvious frustration, I'm now watching everything he does very closely and that's when I spot the problem. His great clodhopping feet are only hitting the accelerator and brake pedals simultaneously! In his defence, the pedals were slightly offset and slightly closer together than they had been on his old Polo, but it was still his clumsy hooves that were causing the problem. Duly acknowledged, feet positioned properly, car (and driver... and passenger) happy again, his beautiful love affair with that car started for real.

He did love it too, too much really. When he decided, after a few months of ownership, that he should try to restore the brilliant red sheen it had when he got it, he duly bought a polishing attachment for his electric drill and set to work with some polish. Unfortunately, he must've picked up some grit on the fleecy contraption and all he succeeded in doing was creating a mass of scratches on the boot. At least he stopped at that!

In fact, the only problem he ever had with the car was that it didn't have power steering, and consequently some of his parking attempts were a joy to behold. At least it gave good outlet to all his hard work in the gym as his strong biceps were required on a regular basis.

When the car eventually expired, he was so sad at having to take it to a scrap dealer. Anyway, the upside was that his next car, a pale green Vauxhall Astra, had power steering and could be steered with one finger, a trick he liked to exhibit to anyone who cared to watch. That car was the only one he ever owned that he could actually remember the registration number of. So SL02 UAC stuck in his mind because, on the day he got it, I pointed out that it described him perfectly – **SL0**(w) **2**(to) **U**nderstand **A**ny **C**ar. That tickled him and so, very late in life, my dad finally appreciated the usefulness of mnemonics. If only it had happened years ago.

He was once stopped by the police, while he was driving home from work late at night, because one of his lights was out. They went through the old, "Is this your car, sir?" routine, and when they asked him his registration number, he promptly rattled off the one from the car he'd had before. He saw the policeman at the front of his car shake his head so he said, "Oh no, that was the last one," and trotted out another old number.

Cue the same shake of the head followed by, "Can you step out of the car, sir?"

Anyway, it all eventually resolved itself without the need for handcuffs but was hugely amusing for us when he recounted the tale.

But enough about cars already – that digression has just catapulted us forward around 50 years! Back to the story…

The other stuff I can remember about those pre-school years may not be genuine memories. You know how sometimes if you've heard stories often enough, particularly when you're young, they kind of stick and then you think they're actual memories? Or is that just me?

One story, from when I was obviously too young to remember but that I heard often enough over the years from my parents, was about the panic I induced in my mum one day when I took a giant gulp of some potentially poisonous liquid that had been prescribed by the doctor for painting lightly on my tongue or gums in order to clear up some minor ailment. On phoning the doctor for advice she was instructed to make me drink salty water in an attempt to make me sick, then to get me to hospital without delay to have my stomach pumped.

Maybe it's just as well I don't remember this actual event as it sounds both gruesome and terrifying. However, I was clearly quite robust and managed to survive, apparently without any ill effects, though I'm sure it would've taken Mum longer to recover!

I *think* I can remember, in a really hazy, grainy, black-and-white kind of way, being in my grandparents' house and my Auntie Bette playing a banjo, but they moved from there when I was only two or three years old – am I really remembering that event, or was it just an often-recounted family story alongside old photographs? Who knows?

Another snapshot of the wee Gordie, from family folk-lore, comes from when I was sitting at the side of the road on the bridge over the railway near our house, locally known as the Smokie Bridge, probably from when steam trains would cloud it over. Apparently, I was sitting there with my wee pal Murray from along the road – his mum must've been within earshot – as this older woman approached and helpfully suggested to him, "Better to keep your legs in a bit, sonny, in case a car goes past."

What a kind thought, and so gently delivered, but before Murray could comply, yours truly allegedly offered his friendly guidance by advising him, "Dinnae listen tae her,

Murray. If ye want tae stick yer legs oot, stick yer legs oot!" – this is probably the first recorded instance of what would later manifest into a fully-fledged disregard for authority and being telt whit tae dae!

Anyway, one absolutely genuine, and precious, memory I have of my pre-school years is of being taken to the cinema to see *Pinocchio* by Tommy and his then girlfriend, and future wife, Pat. Approximately 30 seconds after leaving the house, having just crossed the road, I somehow managed to trip and had to be taken back in to clear away the resultant blood, snot and tears before resuming the expedition! And, bizarrely, I also remember having porridge for supper when we got back!

I can also definitely clearly remember Tommy taking me down to the grassy park area beside Carnoustie Railway Station before tea one evening, taking the stabilisers off my bike and patiently guiding me into riding properly, thus setting me free to cause havoc on two wheels for many years to come. Happy days!

CHAPTER 2

Not too cool for school

(1964–1968)

Unlike now, what with a formalised 3–18 curriculum and all kinds of nanny-state interference over what's best for children, in the mid-1960s our formal socialisation and education pretty much began with day one at primary school. It would be great, particularly for the purposes of this book, if I could recount every detail of that time but, sadly, I can't. Still, what I can remember is more than enough to justify writing this chapter, which is a good thing!

Initially, Mum would've taken me in the morning and collected me at lunchtime, but how long that period lasted is another memory lost in the mists of time. All of my genuine memories revolve around being dropped off by Dad in the morning then walking home for lunch, back to school, then home again. It was around a mile each way, which was quite far for those little legs, but it was just what everyone did. It disturbs me nowadays the way kids are mollycoddled and driven or accompanied everywhere. How are they going to build confidence and independence? I think parents are storing up trouble for the future.

Sometimes, but not often, I would get the bus. If it was a double-decker, the ones with the open door at the back, then our great game was to jump off before the bus had come to a complete halt. That backfired on me big time once when the bus didn't slow down at all at my stop, but I still jumped, meeting the bus stop at around 30 mph in a real *Tom and Jerry* moment! I told you I did my best to test the safety of our small town.

I have no idea what would've made the difference, what the deciding factor was between walking or bus, though the bus-stop incident may have loomed large, but the norm was to walk. Or run…

My first best friend, Stuart Johnstone, was a great runner, even in a school cap and trench coat – not the best look when combined with grey shorts! I never had a trench coat, thankfully, but I did have the cap, for a wee while anyway – with my general demeanour towards authority, even at that tender age, this kind of militaristic hangover was never destined to last. And we were supposed to stand to attention, remove our caps and salute should we ever see the Headmaster, a venerable old retired Colonel or something like that. Even if we were in the middle of town and he drove past. Everyone recognised his car, though I can't remember exactly why, though I am tempted to say it may have been a Rolls or a Bentley, or something big and prestigious anyway.

Mum remarked one day that Stuart looked very like his dad, a local bank manager. Deadpan, and with an effortlessly ironic humour that I like to think has developed well over the years, I replied, seriously, "No he's not – he's not bald." Anyway, we used to race each other to his house, which was probably about halfway. Boy, he was fast, but I won my fair share.

One lunchtime, just after leaving Stuart, a car pulled up and a stranger invited me in. But, as I had been very well trained by my parents, and was therefore prepared for just such an event, I refused politely before running home. What was that all about?

I say well trained but that wasn't the phrase springing to my parents' minds when I returned home one day with a cundie in my school bag! For non-Scots reading this, a cundie is a metal drain cover. Whatever the language, it still makes no sense – why did I bring it home? I have no idea, but when Dad came home he made me retrace my steps until we found a drain without a cover and said cundie was reunited with what we assumed was its hole!

Another time, after leaving Stuart, I was idly kicking stones, probably pretending I was Ian Mitchell or Finn Dossing (United heroes of the time), when I was actually bundled into a stranger's car. But this stranger was furious, intent only on taking me home to exact retribution for "throwing stones at his car". Honest, guv, I wasn't. I didn't even see the car – I was too busy volleying a chuckie into the top corner of an imaginary goal.

Mum soon sent him off with a flea in his ear – how dare he pick up her son, etc., etc. After he left though, "Wait till your father gets home" was only one of the many things assaulting my ear.

School was good. I enjoyed lessons, had loads of friends and spent every spare moment playing football. What was not to like? It all came easily. I was a clever wee boy, probably partly innately and partly fuelled by my excellent reading and counting initiation by my mum. Strange how educational practices change though – I can remember being dragged through from my Primary 1 (P1) class into a P2 or P3 group and being made to read something to them. No explanation, and no choice. Then I had to stand there while their teacher lambasted them for not being able to read as well as this young child! I have no idea what was going through their minds, and I'm sure I was pretty dischuffed too. What educational theory was being followed there? Not any credible one, that's for sure.

Twice a week, Tuesday and Thursday, I would meet my mum at the school bus stop and we would head off to Dundee. On a Tuesday it was to visit her friend Iris, who happened to work with Dad, and on a Thursday it was to visit Gran Craigie, my dad's mum.

On the Tuesday, we would usually walk around a few shops in Dundee city centre before getting another bus up to Iris's house on the Hilltown. We used to go to the City Arcade a lot, as the second bus left from the terminus just outside. The arcade under the Caird Hall has long gone, as has the bus stance, replaced by the monstrosity that was Tayside House, which itself has now been demolished as part of the Dundee Waterfront Project.

Like most kids I wouldn't really be paying too much attention to whatever Mum was looking at, just idly looking at anything and everything that caught my eye.

One time when I must've been particularly bored or distracted, I just wandered out of the arcade following Mum, got on the bus with her and sat down beside her waiting for the conductor. When he arrived and asked for my fare I just pointed at my mum and then realised in horror that it wasn't her – I'd just followed some random woman in a blue coat out of the arcade and onto the bus. Well, nobody really bothered, never mind panicked, and I just calmly got off and headed back to the arcade to find Mum. Except, she wasn't there. Now, at this point there may have been a mild element of panic... certainly for Mum. I, however, displaying a maturity beyond my tender years, calmly walked through the city centre to Dad's office and presented myself. He phoned Iris, Mum was there, everybody relaxed and... I never wandered off again!

One other strange memory I have from those biweekly bus journeys to Dundee is of sitting on the bus, staring at the heavily condensated window and, for reasons still unknown, thinking about the year 2000. And how I would be 41... great arithmetical ability, but why was I thinking about that? Who knows? The year 2000 seemed exotic, or something, I suppose.

The other thing I used to do to pass the time on the journey was to fantasise about running along the walls and hedges of the houses alongside the road, jumping over gates and swinging round lamp posts. I think I may actually have invented parkour in my own wee mind before anyone else had even thought of it!

So P1 and P2 passed without too many outstanding memories, apart from the reading torture mentioned earlier. Oh, but the end of P1 did bring about my stage debut – I played the front half of a windmill in the school concert in our local community centre, the Beach Hall! I'm sure Mum and Dad were extremely proud of their floury-faced wee angel, though I have no recollection of what the point of the sketch was. But I do remember that I won a prize at the end of each year, mainly because I've still got the books!

At the end of P1 I received a copy of *Dick Whittington*, which includes the wonderfully innocent line "I showed your pussy to the King and Queen", while the end of P2 was marked by an Enid Blyton title, *Adventure Stories*. The fact that Scottish schoolchildren were the innocent victims of this kind of colonial brainwashing – tales of the Lord Mayor of London and jolly hockey sticks English boarding schools presented as the norm – is something that really appals me.

Anyway, on a happier vibe, I also remember that I liked my teacher, Miss Smith – it wasn't her that dragged me next door, though she must've sanctioned it.

One day we had a new boy in the class. That was always a strange event in a school, a new pupil's arrival. In her eagerness to have the new kid, Colin, accepted, as we were heading out for playtime she said, "Everybody play with Colin." Even at that young age it struck me as a ridiculous thing to say. How exactly could everybody play with Colin?

Mind you, at a later stage playing with Colin nearly had disastrous, if not terminal, consequences for young Gordie.

One day, possibly a Sunday, I set off to visit said Colin at his home, on my little bike (stabilisers by now a distant memory thanks to my big brother) with my prized Johnny Seven gun casually slung over my shoulder. On my return, I must've experienced some form of equipment malfunction as I discovered, far too late to do anything about it, that I couldn't actually operate the brakes while balancing the Johnny Seven gun. This came to light as I descended Lochty Street, which is quite steep towards the bottom where it meets Carnoustie's main street.

Failure to engage the brakes meant I shot straight across the main road and was only brought to a halt by the helpful intervention of the wall of the Kinloch Arms Hotel, as I crashed straight into it! Checking that I was OK, the bike was OK, and the Johnny Seven gun was OK, though not necessarily in that order, I resumed my journey home, giving very little thought as to "what if...?" Only in later years, as Carnoustie's traffic became heavier, did I belatedly reflect on my good fortune at having avoided being obliterated by a car or a bus. Let's face it, I don't think old Johnny Seven was going to offer much protection!

The other significant memory from those early school-days is that we had one boy in our class, John, who had been born with a hole in his heart, which was a really big deal at that time. That's not to trivialise his condition at all, just that times change and procedures become more routine. John had to stay in at playtime, and I think someone always stayed with him to keep him company. Usually a girl, I think, or one of the strange guys who didn't like football! Of course, immediately before playtime we all got our milk – one of the finest primary-school rituals until it was killed off by the Antichrist who was Margaret Thatcher, horrible woman! It was great for most of the year, but on the odd warm Scottish day the milk tasted awful as it was, at best, lukewarm. Maybe just my taste, but I hated that. Also, contrary to most folk, I hated it if it had cream on top. Yuch!

For P3 we moved across the corridor and took up residence with Mrs Ferrier, an older, greyer, stricter lady who neverthe-less I have fond memories of. Again, I don't recall much detail from any of the learning and teaching of that year, but I do remember vividly that it coincided with United meeting, and beating, Barcelona for the first time in European competition. I may mention again later, probably several times, my belief that United's 100% record against the mighty Barça in competitive games is unrivalled – played four, won four...

The reason I remember it was that year was because I remember writing a story about the game in class. Dad used to call one of our players, Ian Mitchell, the golden boy, and, being entirely trusting of my dad, I thought this was an official nickname. It was actually just his way of describing how he thought Mitch was perhaps rated above his abilities! Anyhow, my story contained mention of "Golden Boy" Mitchell and, continuing the theme naïvely, I came up with "Wonder Boy" Hainey, who was actually Billy Hainey. Billy wasn't at United too long, but he does have "scored against Barcelona – twice!" on his footballing CV. I'd take that.

More important than the story, I remember the game. United's biggest ever crowd, officially 28,500 but probably more, crammed into Tannadice. We couldn't get near the bit we usually stood at and ended up right at the front of the area that is now the Jim McLean Stand. It was electric, it was 16 November 1966, and I was seven years old. This was by a country mile the most people I had ever seen in one place, and the biggest game of football I had seen.

There had been great excitement leading up to the game. It was United's first home European tie and it was against the holders, CF Barcelona, one of the game's giants. Even the "CF" seemed exotic! And we were leading since, two weeks earlier, we had beaten them 2–1 on their own ground, the legendary Camp Nou.

The *Evening Telegraph* had printed a special souvenir magazine that doubled as a programme, and I devoured that. I must've read every word and pored over every picture, advert, statistic, whatever, a million times. And we won... 2–0. Incredible. We had beaten the holders 4–1 on aggregate.

Many, many years later I dragged my wife around the museum at the Camp Nou, where Barça's history is exhibited in minute detail. Only a Dundee United fan would spot the evidence of those games in 1966, as Barcelona have apparently tried to erase it from their memory. But there is, or at least was when we visited, a historical timeline mural or chart dotted around the museum that recounts the events of each year since their formation in 1899 – 1966 simply says something like "not a good year". I'm sure I read something years ago where a Barça director attributed the club's resurgence to Dundee United as losing to a club "like that" made them realise things had to change. Cheeky sod! Twenty years later, we'd be back to gub them again!

Remember those digressions I warned you about? There was another one!

Actually, here's another! That year also saw the first holiday I can remember. It may have actually been our first ever because Dad was always keen to relate how the (even) younger Gordon had had a kind of sixth sense about his dad's impending holiday times, and always managed to come down with measles or chickenpox or some such infectious ailment immediately prior to his holidays, thus scuppering any chance of going away. By now however I was clearly made of sterner stuff, having built up my resistance through exposure to all sorts at school, like you do, and so we were ready for a big adventure – Nairn.

At the time, Nairn was probably the Moray Coast's equivalent of Carnoustie, famous as a holiday town with beaches and a golf course. Not as good as Carnoustie, clearly, but exciting nonetheless, and an awfully long way away to a young child.

We set off on the day of the World Cup Final – you know, the one that was only won due to some myopic officiating? Let's be quite clear on this one for any Sassenachs stumbling across this tale – THE BALL DID NOT CROSS THE LINE! So, just as Denis Law famously spent the afternoon of 30 July 1966 on the golf course, so the Craigie clan spent it travelling the 200 miles or so up to Nairn.

I'd never been on a journey that long and was well bored by the end. I'm certain there must've been many "are we nearly there yet" moments, but finally we arrived around teatime on a beautiful sunny day and we discovered who had won the World Cup. Despite my love of football, my horizons had not extended much beyond Tannadice Park at this stage therefore, all joking aside, England's victory really didn't register with me emotionally. And since live TV coverage was extremely rare, not seeing it was of absolutely no consequence to me. That awareness, of football life beyond Tannadice, took another two years to come about, so stick with it...

The reason Nairn was the chosen destination was because one of Dad's friends owned a hotel there, the Victoria Arms Hotel. This then was to become our holiday destination of choice for around the next 12 years.

On arrival, it was like we entered some sort of twilight zone. The owner, Alec, obviously worked all day and only knocked off after the bars were closed and all the cleaning up etc. was completed, around midnight. So that was when he and Dad would get together and drink coffee and put the world to rights deep into the early hours. The hotel was a typical old Victorian Scottish hotel of its time. Dark, creaky, two toilets and one bathroom shared between around ten bedrooms – all mod–cons! We usually slept in a bedroom with one double and one single bed. If the hotel was otherwise full we would be decanted to the owner's living quarters up in the attic!

Mum would get annoyed at Dad not coming to bed until around 4 or 5 a.m. – I never noticed. Then, me and her would be up around 8–8.30 a.m. and go down for breakfast. I would always have poached eggs on toast – I loved that! If we were lucky, Dad might make it down just before 10 a.m. – important, as, with standard Scottish hospitality etiquette of the time, breakfast stopped at 10 a.m. on the dot – but if he'd been particularly late getting to bed, then he wouldn't make it at all.

Shortly after breakfast me and Mum would head off into downtown Nairn, window-shopping or popping into some of the wee knick-knack shops as we went, but pretty much heading straight to a coffee shop at the bottom of the road. Oh, we knew how to live the high life! Dad would eventually join us, sometime after 11 a.m., but by then it'd be just about time for lunch. So we'd wander back to the hotel, but it was this holiday that really exposed my fussy eating habits as I would never eat any of the lunchtime fare. Eventually my parents gave up cajoling me and it was agreed that I could miss lunch and survive on breakfast and tea, and whatever coffee shops or ice-cream parlours we visited in between.

Morganti's was one of our regular haunts, where I always had what was then called an iced drink but is now usually referred to as an ice-cream float – basically some form of fizzy drink with ice cream in it. I even started a revolution by asking for the drink to be Coca-Cola. Now, a Coke Float would eventually become quite common, but when we were frequenting Morganti's I was looked on very strangely for asking for that particular combination. I always thought I was ahead of my time!

OK, that's enough of the Nairn digression, for now.

Between the end of P3 and the start of P4 there was the small matter, and excitement, of my brother's wedding. I've got fairly random memories of the build-up, the day itself and the aftermath. For instance, I can remember clearly being forced to wear a green suit, complete with short trousers and sandals – the shorts meant that my scratched legs from jumping through a rose bush in the week leading up to the wedding are particularly highlighted in the photos. Mum was not amused!

After the ceremony, the reception was held in the Station Hotel and I can remember that the best man's speech was hilarious, though I have absolutely no memory why! I also can't explain why I don't remember the obvious change in our domestic circumstances after the wedding – you'd think your brother leaving home, getting the bedroom (indeed the bed!) to yourself, and all that sort of stuff would leave something floating about in your brain... but, nope, I got nothing! What I do remember is the date – 8 July 1967. Why? Because I remember the excitement of seeing in *The Courier* that United had drawn 2–2 with Wolves while playing under the guise of Dallas Tornado in the North American Soccer League! Football trumps all!

Once the excitement of the wedding was out of the way, Tommy and Pat set off on their exotic honeymoon – a tandem trip up north! Fair play though, they made it up to just outside Elgin, which is a fair old distance, especially on a "bicycle built for two". Neither of them had previously shown any interest in cycling, so this choice seemed a wee bit unusual, though the fact that they never repeated the feat is probably less so!

When they returned, they moved into their first house, the tenement flat in Dundee that had previously been occupied by my Auntie Pat before they moved to Canada – nothing like keeping it in the family, eh? Less exciting for my brother was the fact that he may have moved into his new house with his new bride, but he had nae job! His wedding present from his employer was to be shown the door, as he had finished his time and they didn't need another journeyman. It probably only took a few weeks before he was back at his tools but, as his enforced break coincided with my summer holidays, the bonus for me was that I was packed off on the bus to Dundee a couple of times that summer to spend time with him.

I remember two occasions – both times he met me at the bus station, then we walked to a park to kick a ball about for a wee while before walking to his house to wait for Dad to collect me in the evening. One time our park of choice was Dudhope Park, and the other was Magdalen Green. I also remember the excitement of being presented with a whole Mars Bar all to myself, and the poignancy of listening to Tommy's records in his new house, records I was familiar with from our old bedroom in Carnoustie. He'd just bought a new single, the Bee Gees' number-one hit, "Massachusetts", which turned out to be the last single he ever bought. Such was the reality of married life!

After the summer holidays, the move to P4 meant a move, literally, up the school. P1, P2 and P3 were housed in the Infants' corridor and for P4 we moved into another linked block. The way the classes were arranged meant that, in our year at least, there was an A and a B stream. This was completely random and was neither ability nor alphabetically based. P4B was the first time I really remember much about this distinction, and the element of competition that came with it.

Our classroom adjoined that of 4A and at some point during the year Mrs Scott permitted me to go through to their classroom to issue a challenge. I don't have a clue how it came about, or why I was the ringleader, but the challenge was for an Us v Them, 4B v 4A football match to be played at Pitskelly Park one afternoon after school. Our team got changed at one of our classmate's gran's house for some reason, even though it was about a mile from the park, then we duly marched along there and thrashed them on a beautifully sunny late spring/early summer afternoon.

I don't remember the final score or the goalscorers – I know I was definitely one of them – but we scubbed 4A anyway, and I'm pretty certain double figures were involved!

We repeated the exercise again later in the year, and we won again, but I really have no recollection of any of the details other than the great satisfaction of organising, and the excitement of playing in, the games, and winning.

With hindsight, those two matches would be the first I ever played in on a full-size football pitch, 11v11. Normally it was just the old jackets-for-goalposts arrangement in the park, apart from every Sunday when a group of us would descend on The Rec – technically, I suppose, ascend, as it was uphill! – to play 6v6 or 7v7, depending on who turned up, on a hockey pitch! It was semi-organised as it was two older boys, Brian and Tony, who organised the games and the squads were pretty much settled – I was in Brian's team – with only the occasional floater or temporary transfer to even up the sides if somebody didn't turn up.

If we had odd numbers then the numerically disadvantaged team had the luxury of nominating rushing keeper, which meant that the goalie could also play outfield, scampering back between the sticks when possession was lost. We used to turn up early afternoon, probably around two-ish, then play until it got dark, or I should emphasise too dark, as after October we needed the light from the streetlamps in Carlogie Road/Newton Road to let us see anything after around 3.30! Afterwards I would cycle home in time for tea, with Mum and Dad completely unconcerned that they hadn't seen me for three hours or more – happy days indeed!

The other great memory of that school year is my first recollection of live televised football. We – a bunch of the usual suspects – were all playing football in the cul-de-sac of the housing scheme just up the road from our house when, probably around 7.45 p.m., someone shouted, "The game starts soon," or something like that. Anyway, in my mind's eye I can still see us all scattering in different directions homewards at high speed. For me, it was around 250 yards around the corner and along the road, but I was back in plenty time for the build-up. Not exactly the full Sky Sports type of introduction that we're now so accustomed to at that time, just Kenneth Wolstenholme earnestly setting the scene in the few minutes before kick-off. Then, the main event, in glorious black and white: Manchester United v Benfica in the 1968 European Cup Final.

That was also the night that George Best was firmly established as my football hero, as he ran Benfica ragged and scored a fantastic goal as United won 4–1, finally achieving Matt Busby's European dream. I still have my scrapbook from back then, and all the reports and photos from *The Courier* are just about outlasting the faded Sellotape (other brands of sticky tape are available) that's loosely holding them in place.

Mrs Scott was a great teacher. She was really strict though, but so encouraging and aware of each of us as individuals. She gave us all a Christmas present, just a wee notebook, inscribed, "With best wishes, Elizabeth Scott", but what a lovely gesture. And imagine a teacher having a first name – who knew?

I used that notebook to record the scores and developing league table in the Craigie family *Casdon Soccer* league. *Casdon Soccer* was a table football game, endorsed by Bobby Charlton, no less, which had arrived in our house as a Christmas gift, presumably in 1967 as that would tie in with the notebook! It consisted of a glorious slab of lurid-green plastic with a red team and a white team of flipper-equipped players which were controlled by two circular knobs in each corner. Hours of fun for all the family, and I won the league, of course. According to the notebook, which I still have, most of the games appeared to be between me and Mum. By this time my brother had left the house, so the few games between us are recorded as friendlies, and as Dad never got in from work early enough due to his bin-polishing habit, there was a huge fixture backlog going on. So the league was a bit repetitive, but then a league mainly contested by only two sides ain't exactly unusual in Scotland, is it?

The housing scheme I mentioned a couple of paragraphs ago was, by this time, a regular haunt. For me, the usual access was via a hole in the hedge of the house next to the church then climbing over a wall, though, to be fair, I could just as easily have walked around the corner! As the scheme developed over a few years, so the possibilities for youthful entertainment developed. Each new stage brought half-built houses to play in and new friends to the newly completed houses. Right in the middle there was a playpark – I say playpark as that was its official designation, though it was really just a rutted field for all us kids to congregate legitimately in at the beginning.

One of the boys who lived just behind the park was a very keen, and very good, golfer and would often be seen practising his swing or hitting a few practice balls. I had the severe misfortune to be standing too close to his backswing on one occasion and felt the full force of his three-wood right above my eye! My great good fortune was that it wasn't an inch lower or I'd be writing this while peering through one eye! Oh the sairness! By the time I arrived home a great throbbing tennis-ball-like swelling had appeared above my tears and snot, and Mum whisked me off to the doctor. Thankfully, there was no great harm done, I learned another useful life lesson... and I don't think I even got a day off school!

As P4 meandered to its conclusion the first elements of doubt and unrest would enter my young mind. We were moving. Not just to P5, but to P5 in another school. In fact, we – the Craigie family – were moving lock, stock and barrel. It had been coming for ages but had never quite seemed real.

For the past couple of years I had accompanied Mum and Dad on increasingly regular house viewings as they mulled over returning to live in Dundee. Unlike nowadays, the child was never consulted. I know what my opinion would've been – to stay where we were – but my view was irrelevant. Apparently, Mum had never settled in Carnoustie, which was news to me. She didn't know anyone, nobody spoke to her, she was still an outsider after seven years etc., etc., and, basically, missed her old life in Dundee. So the inevitable came to pass and we headed off for the great adventure, for me anyway, of living somewhere other than Carnoustie – 9 Duff Street, Dundee was to be my new home, and I was about to, reluctantly, become a city boy…

CHAPTER 3

Return ticket to Dundee please

(1968-1969)

… for a year anyway! OK, let the plot develop…

So, we upped sticks and headed for the beautiful Maryfield district of Dundee. Our new semi-detached Victorian villa was about twice the size of our Carnoustie bungalow – and that was just on the ground floor – and, instead of sharing a bedroom like I had up until the previous year, I had a choice of bedrooms! My commute, also known as my walk to school, had reduced from one mile to just over half a mile and our beloved Tannadice Park was only a further 300 yards on from that school. Paradise. Or not. Anyway, we pitched up there in the summer of 1968.

Little Gordie no-mates had to amuse himself for the whole of the summer holidays, which mainly, as I recall, consisted of watching the Mexico Olympics on TV. It was a good one to get interested in too, with all the black power stuff going on and whatnot. I organised myself a wee Olympics project, which basically involved writing stories and drawing

Olympic rings and medal tables in an old jotter. I also set off to Tannadice on my own one day and, on finding the gates open, went in for a mosey around. I'd never seen the ground empty, so this was exciting. I was really surprised though to find that it wasn't actually completely empty, as there was a photographer taking photos of a player wearing a giant sombrero. Except he wasn't one of ours, he was one of theirs, the mob across the road, Dundee! I never did find out why...

The six or seven weeks flew (?) past and I was finally released from captivity to become the latest entrant to Clepington Primary School, the Cleppie. And yes, now I was the new boy! Thankfully, the lovely Miss Abbott did not encourage anyone to "play with Gordon" and I was left to find my own feet. Although nothing in particular has registered with me academically speaking from P5, I must've continued to progress well as I was awarded a prize at the end of the year, a copy of the *Children's Encyclopedia of Knowledge, Book of Achievement*.

Digression time, again... finding my own feet during this year in particular was not the most pleasant of experiences for the young Gordie. I'm sure I'd been already suffering previously, but this was the year it really kicked in with a vengeance – athlete's foot. Big time. It was cruel.

You know when you see dogs with worms scraping their backsides along the ground for relief? Doesn't help athlete's foot! Neither do nylon socks, which were standard issue at the time.

I took to developing my own remedies which, as is the way of these things, only served to make things worse in the long run. You see, I quickly realised that my feet were at their most painful when I'd just got up and the skin was dry and brittle. All of the cracks – and, believe me, there were loads of them – were excruciatingly painful. But I sussed out that when my skin got moist, whether through sweat or other means, everything flexed up a little and the pain subsided. You've never seen a boy keener to wear wellies!

If I didn't have the wellies on to work up a sweat, and let's be honest, even in north-east Scotland there are very few days that actually require wellies in a city, then I had to either run about like crazy, balancing out the initial agony against the upcoming pay-off of moistly flexible skin, or I had to take extreme measures. It may not often be wet enough for wellies, but it is very often wet. Which means puddles. Now, obviously, any medical practitioner will advise that any treatment for athlete's foot is best accompanied by keeping the feet dry. But they weren't suffering the pain.

Anyway, after the ubiquitous Whitfield's Ointment had finally been exposed as a non-remedy for my particular situation, our new doctor prescribed some evil-looking purple crystals – potassium permanganate, apparently – with which to bathe the feet nightly, turning them foully purple in the process. But it worked, to an extent, and although not to be fully cured for many, many years, it was never quite as bad again.

OK, those of a nervous disposition can start reading again as the gruesome exposition of my foostie tootsies is now well and truly over!

On my first or second day at school some of my new classmates suggested meeting up to play football that evening at Caird Park. Now, bearing in mind that Caird Park was approximately 400 yards from my house in Duff Street, nobody thought they should explain to the new boy exactly where it was, and why would they? And the new boy, much as he still would now, didn't bother checking as he knew where he was going. You think?

After tea, I jumped on my bike and pedalled off towards Caird Park, out of Duff Street, right into Clepington Road then a quick left to go down Forfar Road, then left along the Kingsway, Dundee's dual carriageway outer ring road, until I arrived at my destination about one and a half miles away to find... nobody, because that's not Caird Park, it's Downfield Park! I'd already passed Caird Park about the same one and a half miles back, and was to pass it again as I mooched back home feeling totally deflated. I don't remember but I'm sure the boys had a good laugh when I explained my non-appearance the next day.

That year was significant for two events, one national and one a wee bit more local. The national one was the experiment with British Summer Time (BST). It's back on the agenda as I write this, this time mainly due to Brexit and the British Nationalist obsession with "taking back control" or some such nonsense, but I don't really know what all the fuss is. It was OK. Yes, we went to school in the dark but it was no problem. Quite often it's dark in the morning anyway in Scotland, sometimes all day in fact. OK, I know that's me being flippant but I really don't think it mattered to us. I don't particularly remember it being lighter for longer in the afternoon, but it must've been. I'd prefer that anyway, then and now.

Schoolchildren were all to be issued with either a reflective vest or armbands. I don't remember which I had, but that's irrelevant anyway as I do know for an absolute fact that I didn't wear either. How hard is it to walk to school? How hard is it to look right, look left, look right again? What did I say about mollycoddling? If kids can't walk to school and negotiate roads by the time they're nine or ten then shame on their parents. And I know farmers say it'll cause them problems but I just don't get that – can their coos and sheep tell the time? I know it means they'll have to adjust the time that they do certain things by an hour one way or another, but is that really such a big deal? Anyway, that's that particular rant over, for now.

The event of more local significance that happened involved me turning up at school one morning during that particular BST experiment, when it was pitch black, to witness flames shooting out of the Cleppie's roof. So maybe not totally pitch black then. Inspector Clouseau here took one look, deduced the school was on fire and unlikely to be accepting visitors anytime soon, so decided to head home.

Arriving back around half an hour after I'd left I casually informed Mum that the school was on fire and she said something like, "Oh, is it?" Then I just got on with enjoying our bonus day off. Except it wasn't an *official* day off, as I discovered when I returned next day and was duly belted for having gone home without permission, an injustice that still rankles with me, despite my wife's best arguments that the teachers couldn't be certain everybody was safe if people like me had just wandered off. I'm not having that, it was an injustice... said Calimero!

That was the first time I had been given the belt, though it was not to be the last in my primary school career, the other occasion also being at that school and, loosely, fire related too, as we shall see shortly. That the school was open for business as usual the day after a major fire seems quite incredible in today's terms. What is totally unbelievable is what business as usual meant.

Our classroom happened to be on the top floor of the four-storey Victorian building and to reach it, after climbing the stairs, we had to literally walk the plank. Now, I'd normally be one of the first to rail against excesses of health and safety but come on. Thirty odd nine-year-olds walking over a plank of wood with four floors of nothingness underneath it? Someone was having a laugh. But we just took it in our stride. Which was just as well really, as one stumble and…

Talking of laughing, the other belting came as a result of my finding something funny at entirely the wrong time. Or at someone else's definition of the wrong time, that someone else just happening to be a sadist with the trappings of power. In keeping with the mainly Victorian buildings at that time, primary schools still adopted the Victorian practice of making the classes line up outside, irrespective of the weather, before being led into the building. That wasn't a concession to health and safety because of the plank by the way — it happened every single day. Woe betide anyone who was late getting into line. Then there would be the ritual screams of "Stand still, be quiet" from some teacher, usually male, who based their entire act on outdated military practices.

Anyway, one day I was caught laughing or smiling at something that was going on and was summoned by a male teacher who I'm not even sure I'd seen before – "Laughing boy, come here." I was then belted without much further explanation, as I recall, as to exactly what my heinous crime had been. Other than laughing, apparently. Inappropriately, apparently. And people wonder where my distaste for authority comes from?

That winter we made paper-chain Christmas decorations at school. This is a significant recollection only because I became obsessed. I vividly recall trooping down to the Stobswell shops after school in search of the coloured, gummed strips of paper from which I would create my masterpieces. And Mum and Dad, God bless'em, dutifully strung the things up all over the house. Talk about being indulged.

Dad got his own back that year though, however inadvertently. We'd always, in my memory, had the same artificial Christmas tree – I've never, before or since, seen another like it – and I loved it. It was probably around four feet high, silver tinsel with permanently attached lights inside plastic globes that looked a bit like practice golf balls with glitter on. Anyway, my parents decided it was time for a change so Dad duly brought back two other artificial trees to choose between. That probably all sounds fine and dandy so far, but the problem with that was that they left the choice to me. Cue the first sign of a serious character flaw that persists to this day…

This was intensely worrying for someone of my sensitive nature, and not wanting to upset or disappoint my parents in any way, I couldn't sleep! It was so hard to decide, which seems crazy now, but it did set a pattern. I was really, genuinely upset by the pressure of choosing, and changed my mind several times, principally because I was constantly trying to second-guess which one they wanted. However, I eventually arrived at a decision – based on what exactly, I have no idea. But a decision was reached, a tree was chosen and slowly, very slowly, my guilt and anguish dissipated and sleep, eventually, returned.

As if all of that wasn't enough for a sensitive young soul to contend with, that turned out to be the Christmas when the innocence of childhood was obliterated once and for all, in a somewhat clumsy fashion it must be said, by my well-meaning father. I had decided that what I would really like to receive as a Christmas gift from Santa was a watch. After much consultation of my mum's *Kays Catalogue* – go on, you did that too – I decided that a particular timepiece bearing the Smiths brand was the one that I had to have.

One wintry evening, I was in the car with Dad and he said something like, "This watch, son, the one you asked Santa for, does it have to be a Smiths?"

I've no idea what I would've responded to this out-of-left-field question with, but whatever it was didn't dissuade my dad from his follow-up: "Would a Kienzle do? They look the same and Kienzle is actually better."

Now, I didn't know one brand of watch from another, and I'd only asked for the Smiths because that was the picture I'd liked best in the *Kays Catalogue* selection. But if my dad said Kienzle was better, then it must be true, so I must've responded in the affirmative as he then followed up with, "And we've got them in stock just now."

I must've looked a little perplexed at this turn of events because he then, gently but firmly, delivered the killer blow: "You do know that Santa Claus isn't real, that it's me and your mum that buy your presents?"

At this point I must've adopted the time-honoured child-being-brave response of something like, "Yeah, of course," while inwardly howling.

"OK, that's good, that's settled then."

We would never speak of this conversation again, especially not on Christmas Day when Santa duly delivered the very same Kienzle watch that'd been languishing on a Wood and Cairns shelf only days before...

I was also ill at some point during that year. I don't remember if it was ever explained to me what was wrong with me, but I did have a fever and was delirious for a good few days. For some unknown reason I spent the entire period in Mum and Dad's bed, so presumably they were in mine? Why? Who knows, and I never thought to ask.

We were in Dundee over the winter of 1968–69, which was the year of the so-called Hong Kong flu outbreak. [*2020 update: This is something I've only discovered during the current COVID-19 pandemic.*] Was I a victim? Again, sadly, there's no one left to confirm or deny, but I wisnae jist no affy weel, I wis affy no weel – Dundee joke!

Not much else of note happened during that year, apart from staring up at the night sky wondering, and worrying, about the fortunes of the Apollo 8 astronauts. Well, I obviously needed something else to worry about!

During that year I probably exchanged around three or four letters with my friend Stuart. He kept me up to date with happenings in Carnoustie, but I have no idea what I offered in return as there wisnae gey much happening in Dundee! I do, however, remember his final letter, after I had told him we were to be returning to Carnoustie, and apart from his excitement he also related how happy some of my other buddies were that I was returning. That was a good feeling. It was also strange in a way because, when we did return to Carnoustie, Stuart and I were never close again – the others kind of replaced him…

Wait, what? Return? Where did that come from? Well, probably just as I was beginning to settle into my new surroundings, in the way that kids generally do, there were domestic undercurrents that I was blissfully unaware of.

Apparently Dad had come home from work one night to find Mum in floods of tears. She didn't know anyone, nobody spoke to her, she was still an outsider etc., etc., and, basically, missed her life in Carnoustie! Mamma mia! Dundee had changed, and she didn't like it.

So, after only a few months of city life, we started on the whole house-hunting thing again – we'd barely unpacked for heaven's sake! But the upshot was that there was nothing else for it but to cash in the return ticket and head back to Carsnootie (as it is often called on account of the residents being perceived as posher than those in Dundee). But not before spending an interesting two weeks, the last two weeks of the school term, living at my aunt's house because our leaving and entry dates weren't synched. I actually got to walk past Tannadice every day for those two weeks, four times a day... and *then* we headed back to Carsnootie.

One of the last school events I can remember before we headed back, however, was an afternoon when the entire school was shepherded down to line the Kingsway in order to wave flags and cheer as the Queen was driven past in her fancy limousine. When the big moment arrived, I was happily playing football with my mates behind the crowds and was blissfully unaware of either her approach or passage until we were all scooped up and returned to school!

Before we move on from season 68/69, it's probably worth mentioning another obsession that kept me going during that sabbatical year – the prospect of actually starting a real football team. I must've been experiencing withdrawal symptoms as I can't actually recall playing more than a couple of times, except for in the playground, during the entire year.

The playground stuff was notable for seldom actually including a ball! Instead, we mainly used a washing-up liquid bottle cut in half, stuffed with paper, then reassembled with the two halves overlapping. Heading was particularly dangerous due to the hard, plastic nozzle, but since it was so difficult to get it off the ground, and it didn't bounce, this was a rare phenomenon!

The quality of the game increased markedly when one of us, probably me, had an ice-cream container in the shape of a ball – nobody else in my peer group today seems to remember this, but some commercial ice-cream maker produced plastic tubs of ice cream in the shape of a football. There was a removable lid which clipped back into place so that, once the contents had been eaten, you were left with a hard, plastic ball, with many of the same downsides as the washing-up liquid creation but at least with the benefit of actually being round! Oh well...

Anyway, after that latest digression, back to the team building...

The team was to be called Austin United – Austin because I had the key fob from my dad's old car with an Austin badge on it (?) and United for more obvious reasons! This whole thing wasn't entirely played out in my own mind either, oh no. Jimmy, another Gordon, Donald, Jeff and Atholl were definitely on board with the planning process, though I recall Atholl's main contribution was to vehemently insist on "silky black shorts"... I'm not even going there!

Some of us ventured down to Baxter Park – I was able to find that easily enough! – one day for a training session (kick about) and to check out the changing facilities (non-existent) in the then semi-derelict pavilion. For some reason it seemed to escape our notice that the park didn't actually boast a football pitch… Anyway, the only significant outcome of that particular escapade was that it was the last time I was knowingly in possession of my football boots – Tuf since you ask and no, that's not a misspelling, but it was the last pair of boots I would have free of commercial influences. Oh, the innocence of the times.

Mind you, if that flight of fancy seems, well, fanciful, it was at least more realistic than the previous time I had visions of starting my own team. I'd actually had a similar thought a couple of years earlier when we were still in Carnoustie. On that occasion I was convinced, in my own wee heid, that I could mark out a full-size football pitch on a grassy area down at the beach near our house. The fact that said grassy area wasn't big enough anyway, and was anything but flat, did not seem to deter me in any significant way. I also had the notion that we could use torches in place of floodlights so we could play at night, and duly requested a torch from Santa that Christmas – well, it was a start! And clearly that had all been prior to the whole Santa Claus thing being exposed as a scam…

But it was to be the return to Carnoustie, and a massive step up in the football boot stakes, that I eagerly looked forward to, back in the summer of '69…

CHAPTER 4

Back in Carsnootie

(1969–1971)

And so it came to pass that we returned to Carnoustie almost exactly one calendar year after leaving. This time, we were swapping the two-floor grandeur of a semi-detached Victorian villa for a much more modest, yet strangely more expensive, two-bedroomed detached bungalow at 23 Millar Street, Carnoustie. The address was Millar Street yet the house was entered via a narrow lane which ran all the way from the Carnoustie House Grounds park to Terrace Road, crossing Yeaman Street, Millar Street, Maule Street and Collier Street on the way. The previous owner was an architect and he had used every little bit of his 1960s modernist design knowledge to transform the inside of the nineteenth-century stone-built house into, well, something a wee bit different that never entirely worked. But it quickly became home, quirks and all, and would remain so for the next 16 years for me – my parents would live happily there for the rest of their lives.

One vivid memory I have of the moving-in day is that of my brother managing to reverse his work's van down the lane – there must've been around an inch of clearance on either side – to safely deliver my parents' pride and joy, their Blaupunkt radiogram. This stereo wonder was the height of chic when they bought it a few years earlier, so they, especially Mum, were distraught when Tommy's "safe" delivery resulted in a deep gouge on one of the doors, presumably caused by some rough edge in the back of his van.

As was the style of the time, the radiogram had two sliding doors with which to access, on the right, the record deck, radio and amplifier controls, while the left housed... err, the built-in cocktail cabinet? That still seems a strange combination to me but it was all the rage in the '60s.

Even more unusual, perhaps, is that my parents were both strictly teetotal, so the bottles of whisky, sherry and advocaat that surrounded the round metal tray with the crystal decanter and sherry glasses – only ever used for bringing in the New Year – were afforded plenty of time to mature in their bottles over the years! Most of the time we only knew they were in there when they started to rattle in response to my turning up the volume on the increasingly frequent occasions that I'd be playing the best of whatever old records were lying around the house.

Anyway, back to moving-in day – I also remember Mum answering the door around an hour after we arrived to find a squad of my old friends eager for me to come out and play football with them. Naturally, I accepted this kind invitation and the last year spent in exile melted away as it seemed like only yesterday that I'd last seen them.

I don't recall any other particular details of that summer holiday – it would've just been more of the same really, whiling away the days playing in the park, football (mainly) but also hide-and-seek, kick-the-can, or going down to the trampolines and tennis courts at Carnoustie beach – and nothing sticks out either about returning to school in the August. I suppose I wasn't really a new boy – I was just the same laddie that everyone remembered from the previous years, so there was no fuss made, everything and everyone was familiar, so it was just back to business as usual.

Once again, my commute had reduced, this time to a mere quarter mile, which was fantastic news. It meant I could pretty much leave home when the first warning school bell rang and still be in time for the real bell – both could be clearly heard from our new house.

Unlike previously, in Ireland Street, I was no longer the furthest flung member of our group, so that meant that all of my closest friends would pass our house en route to school, which in turn meant we could all walk to school together. That was both comforting and enjoyable, and the only thing that made me aware that I'd been away at all was the horrific realisation that, in my absence, formal, organised football had started in the school and I therefore had to reassert my place in the scheme of things from a standing start.

Being an outsider among your mates is a very strange sensation indeed, and although I got myself into the swing almost immediately, the feeling of playing catch-up in the football stakes lasted all year.

Mrs McGregor was our P6 teacher and she was yet another one that definitely fell into the hard but fair category. That year would see the first real outward manifestation of the bolshie side of my nature, maybe inspired by the perceived injustices at Cleppie the previous year – "laughing boy!" – or perhaps I was just growing up?

Anyway, we were all expected to learn to play the recorder as part of our music instruction and, indeed, to buy one. For reasons again well lost in the mists of time, I wasn't having any of that, so during the compulsory recorder lessons a small handful of us musical refuseniks had to go through the motions with a 12-inch ruler in place of the recorder. What a totally ridiculous and pointless exercise! Mind you, I probably made better sounds than some of my mates did with their recorders...

Educationally everything was going well and I had no problems in regaining my customary position at, or around, the top of the class and, therefore, P6 came and went with my order in the grand scheme of things thoroughly re-established for our biggest move yet – to the head of the school, P7.

Awaiting us there was the man who was to become the first outstanding educational influence on the young Gordon, outside of my family of course – Mr Fimister, or as he was universally known (but never within his earshot), Fimmy.

Dave Fimister was quite simply a wonderful teacher. Outwardly hard as nails and not to be crossed, yet kind, very kind actually, funny, interested and interesting. He introduced us to so many things that year, and I'm sure his early adoption of modern individualised teaching methods greatly influenced me in later years.

Every Monday he would sit down with each of us individually to check on our progress over the last week and to hand out that week's assignments. He would detail exactly how much work we were expected to get through in Mathematics, English, Geography, History and probably other subjects that I've forgotten about. First thing each morning, he would tell us what we were going to be doing that day, and he'd then give group or individual lessons while others got on with what had already been set for them. We would have whole class lessons sometimes, but never in subjects like Mathematics or English where the ability range was wide – those lessons were undertaken individually or in very small groups.

Even if he was working with one of us individually he still possessed the uncanny talent of knowing exactly what everyone else in the class was up to, good or bad, while apparently still giving the individual his undivided attention. Nobody got away with anything!

Fimmy also took care of art, music and all sorts of general stuff. In fact, the only outsourcing to a specialist was for PE, although at that time it was called either drill or gym, when we would make the short journey along the main street to the ATC (Air Training Corps) Drill Hall where Mr Simmons would put us through our paces.

Mr Simmons was, to us young children, a fearsome character with an even more fearsome reputation for strict discipline – not a man to be messed with. His real job was actually in the adjoining junior secondary school, so whether his time with us was a blessed relief from coping with obstreperous teenagers or a babysitting nightmare is a moot point!

The ATC hall was always freezing, but irrespective of the time of year us boys were only ever allowed to wear white shorts and white gym shoes (also known as sandshoes, or sannies!) – and woe betide anyone whose kit wasn't clean and, especially, white! The girls had to wear white, or blue, blouses and dark blue shorts to complement their white sannies.

We'll return to Mr Simmons in a later chapter, but his physical education responsibilities were restricted to that gym hall, and it was Dave, and his female P7A counterpart Mrs MacDougall, who supervised our weekly trips to Arbroath Indoor Baths and our swimming lessons...

The bus journeys there and back were just another excuse for an out-of-classroom carry-on, and I always looked forward to them more than the actual swimming. Fimmy did his best to teach us, but while he and many of my classmates were innately capable of swimming like fishes, I was equally capable of sinking like a stone, a quality that I retain to this day! It causes my wife great amusement to witness my attempts at treading water, with my head below the surface of the pool!

Despite that, I am still the proud possessor of a Grade 1 Swimming Certificate which states unequivocally that I could, at least once, "Jump or dive into the pool and swim continuously, without contact with pool wall or floor, for 50 feet, using any stroke or strokes."

What it doesn't say is that I couldn't do it while still breathing! I only managed the feat because, contrary to what the test specifies above, we were allowed to demonstrate our prowess (?) by swimming 25 feet across the pool then 25 feet back, which I was just about able to do on only the two breaths!

Further proof that I was much more capable out of water was the fact that I was able to pass, with ease, my National Cycling Proficiency Certificate and then complete a trio of random awards by also receiving a Certificate of Merit for Distinction in Scottish Literature, from The Burns Federation. So, all in all, not a bad wee collection for one year, but there was bigger and better to come...

Another of Dave's many responsibilities was to manage our school football team, which also involved him cramming five or six of us into his Sunbeam Rapier coupé (or Sunbeam Interceptor as we called it, in homage to the Jenson Interceptor, supercar of the time) while another parent or two, or sometimes even the Heidie, Alex H. Taylor himself, took the rest of the team. We used to fight over who went with Fimmy and I don't recall ever missing out.

As a piece of fairly unrelated trivia, Alex's son David ended up as the Chief Executive of the SFA before progressing to be General Secretary of UEFA then finishing his career as Chief Executive of UEFA's marketing company. The Farfar loon done good!

Our football team was incredible. We were actually undefeated for two entire seasons, comfortably winning the Angus P6 and P7 leagues as well as the Angus School's knockout cup competition. Our team pretty much never changed – in the WM formation of the time we had:

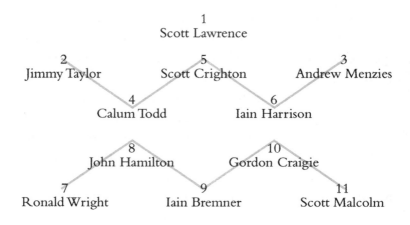

Derek Harrison and Kenny Gourlay were our substitutes, and Alec Potter and Roger Hutchison were our substitute substitutes, but that was back in the day before substitutions happened during a game, so these guys only really got in if someone was ill or injured.

One of our big bits of excitement early that year was being given a say in the new kit. The old blue-and-green-quartered stuff – ancient, heavy, cotton rugby-style shirts hanging around from the old Carnoustie Junior School days – was up for replacement with something more befitting of the new, vibrant Kinloch Primary School. Our school colours were still green and blue but, however it happened, we ended up with bright yellow nylon jerseys, shiny black shorts and red socks. We thought we were absolutely the bees' knees.

Because of my continuing foostie tootsies problem, my parents bought a pair of red socks for me so that I wouldn't threaten the foot health of my teammates through pooling and sharing the fetid fungus! And, on a much more positive note, my particular look was completed by my George Best Stylo Matchmaker boots with the super cool and trendy side lacing. All thoughts of the lost Tufs were well and truly gone as my state-of-the-art boots definitely helped me to be second-top goalscorer behind Iain Bremner, and I laid on most of his goals too! Others may have different memories...

By virtue of being finally at the head of the school we were assigned various duties, like taking it in turns to run around the playground with the handbell to signal the end of playtime and lunchtime. I'm glad that we were allocated this task on a rotation basis as it fair played havoc with our footballing activities!

Despite the fact that one goal consisted of our classroom window, we didn't suffer any breakages during the year. That wasn't a comment on our goalscoring abilities, however – quite the reverse.

Being an old Victorian building the windows were quite far off the ground, with the sill probably a good five feet off the ground. Our shooting accuracy was so good that we seldom went higher than that, which was useful at the other goal too as it was formed by two trees but had a reasonably low wrought-iron fence behind it and shots that were too high would take the ball onto the main road. As we weren't allowed to leave the playground, on the rare occasions that this happened, we would all hang on to the railings eagerly awaiting the next passing pedestrian that we could shout at pleadingly to "please throw our ball back". Thankfully that didn't happen too often.

One of Dave's big contributions to my wider intellectual development came about through his music afternoons. He was a big music fan and, indeed, a highly skilled musician playing trumpet semi-professionally in the East Coast Jazzmen for over 60 years! So Dave had a wide and varied record collection, and he used to bring in a different album each week – though we still called them LPs back then – and force us to listen to the whole thing in silence.

It was probably just a crafty way of him getting some peace and quiet to do some preparation or marking while listening to some of his favourite music, but he did explain to us what it was all about and what we should be listening out for.

One unanticipated outcome for me was that I discovered that I actually did like some classical music – *The Planets* suite by Gustav Holst, for instance, stuck in my mind and now sits nestled in my CD collection.

But the biggie for me was when he absolutely blew my little mind away with the Beatles' album, *Abbey Road*. Now I already loved the Beatles, mainly due to my brother's influence, but everything I knew about them at that time was based on their first two albums and the film *A Hard Day's Night*. All the stuff in between, like *Revolver, Rubber Soul* or even *Sergeant Pepper* had, at this stage in my life, passed me by. But *Abbey Road*, wow!

So impressed was I that it duly made it to the top of my Christmas list that year, whereupon Dad kindly bought me... the Seekers album! Now, I don't know how familiar you are with the relative positions of Australian puppet pop bands vis-à-vis the greatest rock band in history but, apparently, my dad thought they were interchangeable. No, they weren't! Don't get me wrong, I actually do have a secret soft spot for the Seekers now, probably as a result of hearing that album quite a few times, but there really is no contest.

Anyway, that record arrived after another stressful pre-Christmas period for your sensitive chronicler.

That year, probably around late November, with any lingering fantasies of Santa Claus and his little elves long since destroyed, Dad announced that I could have a choice of Christmas present, between a set of golf clubs and a stereo music system. In cold print that actually looks like a more than reasonable choice and what a lucky wee boy I was to have a chance of receiving either of these magnificent gifts. And that's absolutely true. I wasn't, and have never been, spoiled, so that's not the issue here. No, if you recall the trauma caused two years previously when the choice of

Christmas tree was left to yours truly, you might just see what's coming here.

Does he want me to play golf? Up to this point in my life, my only experience of the world-famous championship golf course on my doorstep had consisted of falling in the Barry Burn in front of the eighteenth green!

OK, it's been a wee while since this big a digression, but... I'd been walking over the course with a few friends and, as we were approaching the end of our adventure, I had just walked across the concrete bridge which, significantly, had no sides or guardrails, when one of the others shouted on me to come back. So I turned to walk back but, inexplicably, somebody had apparently moved the bridge and so I plummeted into the depths of the burn, much to the amusement of my amigos – I say "depths", but it must be all of two feet deep at that point.

Anyway, apart from my pride, the only casualty was my hand-knitted jumper, which never regained its original size after its drenching – to say Mum was not best pleased would be a serious understatement when her drookit wee laddie squelched through the front door, though her displeasure was more to do with her shrunken handiwork than any concern for my well-being!

Right, where were we? Oh yes, golf clubs or stereo system, and me trying to second-guess my dad... Or, since he sells stereo stuff and gets excited by new products in that line, does he really want me to go down that route?

Even worse than "What does he want me to do?" is "Will he be upset if...?" It was déjà vu all over again! (That's deliberate, by the way!) Many sleepless nights, and even arguments, followed as I tried to avoid making, or at least relating, a decision. Eventually, probably for reasons as obscure as with the final Christmas tree choice, I plumped for the stereo.

"Are you sure?"

Oh God, I've upset him. He does want me to choose the golf clubs...

Cue more sleepless nights, more heartache... pathetic, really – but, it still happens to this day, which is even more pathetic! Anyway, finally the stereo decision was confirmed – though I seriously still had flashback panic attacks about the golf clubs for many years to come – and it duly arrived on Christmas Day... along with the Seekers album to christen it!

That stereo was absolutely fantastic – record deck, integrated radio/amplifier and floor-standing speakers – the finest Russian engineering of the day clad in a shiny wooden veneer. I'm not being sarcastic there, by the way – the technology was right up there.

Dad had started importing Rigonda radios, TVs and stereos in his business, and Rigonda was putting in a lot of effort trying to break into the UK market. As a result they were offering great prices, and the quality was really, really good. That stereo did sterling service for about the next 12 years, impressing all-comers of both sexes, and I absolutely loved it.

So impressed was my mate Stuart Duncan, Stooge, that he even bought one himself from my dad a year or two later. He bought the smaller model as he wasn't interested in the radio, just the record deck. Stooge decided he had to have one after I blasted his ears off with Sweet's number one single "Blockbuster", impressing him with the special effects, as I called them. Those special effects amounted to nothing more than extreme volume but, since the sound was actually so good compared to what others normally listened on, the effects were pretty special.

Maybe it was the arrival of the stereo system, or maybe it was because of Fimmy stirring a wider musical awakening, but that was the year when music really started to register with me. And I always seemed to like stuff just a wee bit off mainstream. Still chart stuff – what else was I likely to hear in those days? – but usually not what appealed to the majority of my peers. Hence that year saw me getting into Dave Edmunds (*I Hear You Knockin'*), Hotlegs (*Neanderthal Man*) and the Kinks (*Apeman*) while deepening my interest in the Beatles and the first knockings of their respective solo careers. In particular I recall Paul's "Another Day", Ringo's "It Don't Come Easy" and George's "My Sweet Lord", the first single I ever bought.

But the absolute highlight of our P7 year was... the annual Kinloch Primary School Trip to London. Mind you, I nearly missed it due to a lack of communication, and an administrative cock-up, between me and my parents. The deal was, at some point earlier in the school year we all had to decide if we were going to London or not and, if we were, our place would be reserved by the payment of a £2 deposit. £2? I know, ludicrous, isn't it? But, as the cliché goes, that's when £2 was £2. That then left £20 to pay. £20? I know, even more ludicrous!

Our total payment of £22 was to cover the bus from Carnoustie to Dundee Railway Station, the Caledonian Sleeper to London, transport to our hotel, accommodation for three nights, all meals, all transport around London, all entry fees, and the return journey home via sleeper and bus again. For £22 – amazing!

Anyway, having paid the £2 deposit we were given the option of paying £1 per week or just bringing the £20 in on the last week. Can we all see where this is heading? My family opted for the £20-at-the-end route, but when it came to the last week, we had all forgotten to do anything about it. I'm sure there was even more than one last week as, clearly, the school had been here before and knew some stupid so-and-so would forget.

However, on the very *last* last week, the Craigie family had still forgotten! Cue panic in the classroom on the decisive morning, so the young Gordie escaped from the school grounds at playtime, ran home and was fortunate to (a) find his Mum was in, (b) find that she actually had £20 to hand over, and (c) get back to school before the bell rang again without anyone official noticing he'd left. A close shave indeed but maybe a lesson learned?

Unsurprisingly not as this was not to be the last act of brinkmanship from myself, though they didn't all turn out as successful as this one.

So, cometh the day and we all trooped along to the car park opposite the school on a fine spring Monday evening to haul our luggage aboard the bus headed for Dundee. I think the sheer excitement took away any chance of tears as we waved our goodbyes and we set off on our great adventure.

The sleeper journey was a riot. I shared with Iain Bremner, I think, but there was very little sleeping done – it was far more entertaining to run up and down the corridor, trying to avoid train guards and teachers, or nip in and out the adjoining sleeper.

Despite our best efforts we made it in one piece and probably went straight to our hotel to dump the cases and have breakfast. The hotel, or glorified B&B, was actually fairly grotty and the breakfast was in a similarly grotty building over the road. There were five or six of us in each bedroom, which led to plenty of high jinks, as you might imagine.

At some point during the week we had an unexpected visitor to our room – my dad! Sheer coincidence apparently, but he was in London that same week for a trade show so came round to check on his wee boy. He hadn't let on beforehand so it was definitely a surprise.

We did all the obvious touristy stuff – Tower of London, Buckingham Palace, St Paul's Cathedral, Cutty Sark, Greenwich, History Museum, even Heathrow Airport! When we went to the Houses of Parliament, we were given a tour by our Angus constituency MP, the splendidly double-barrelled Tory Jock Bruce-Gardyne. My political affiliations had just started to stir, and he most certainly wasn't of my persuasion. I was chosen, or was volunteered, to read something in the empty chamber and was presented with a copy of the previous day's *Hansard* for my efforts.

I imagine we were probably packed off to our rooms quite early on the first night, after all the travelling, excitement and a full day of sightseeing, but on the second evening we went to the Victoria Palace Theatre to see *The Black and White Minstrel Show*. Different times indeed.

We actually had a choice of things to do on the third and final night, and the majority vote was for us to visit Battersea Dog's Home but sadly, for some reason never communicated to us, we didn't go and no substitute was arranged. Another evening of mayhem in the room then...

Despite the fact that we were only in London for four full days, that was clearly enough time to send postcards home and… I still have them! The words of wisdom I sent to my mum were, "Having a nice time. Weather marvellous. Wish you were here to enjoy it too. See you Saturday." Bless, I'm tearing up here. I sent similar sentiments to my dad, except for the addition of, "Don't need to tell you much about the weather as you were here." Ever the wordsmith!

The sleeper journey back was probably a whole lot quieter than the one down, and we finally rolled into the car park in Carnoustie around 6 a.m. on Saturday morning. In stark contrast to the busy scene on the Monday evening when we had left, the car park was pretty much deserted. Not many parents had come to collect their offspring, and mine certainly hadn't! So I meandered up to our house – without a key as nobody had thought that far ahead – and, having wandered around peering in all the windows looking for signs of life, concluded I'd have to chap on Mum and Dad's bedroom window to get them to let me in. They weren't best pleased, but my alternatives were rather limited unless they'd expected me to sit in the garden for another three or four hours until they got up.

One of our great adventure playgrounds during this year was the building site of the new Carnoustie High School, which was due to open just in time to herald our year's arrival at secondary school. Site security then wasn't what it is now, and we regularly used to go up there and clamber about as far as the top (fourth) floor. In fact, there would usually be several groups going around, and one time I recall one of our number dislodging a hammer, accidentally I think, while we were on the top floor and hearing a yell as it narrowly missed someone else trailing around the ground floor.

One lunchtime the whole of Carnoustie came to a halt when a massive explosion was heard all over the town. It turned out that some tank at the site had exploded. Thankfully no one was injured, and I don't think it set the work back much, but it did provide a talking point for a few days in our sleepy wee town.

Another building site, much smaller in scale, was the scene of my only real physical calamity of that year. On the way home from school, for a few months we used to take a shortcut through the garden of a house being built between Terrace Road and Collier Street. No great danger obvious in that but one lunchtime, as I ran through the garden, I had the great misfortune to meet a bee flying in exactly the opposite direction. The bee was not best pleased and, clearly possessing much quicker reactions than me, exacted retribution by instantly stinging me... on the eyelid! Ouch!

Around two minutes later, no doubt crying profusely from my other eye, I rushed into the house to announce my accident to Mum who, instantly and calmly, ushered me back out of the house and down to the local pharmacist. I suppose an antihistamine was administered, I don't recall, but I did get the bonus of an afternoon off while my tennis-ball eyelid slowly subsided. Golf clubs? Bees? Kids, eh?

Apart from football, music, foreign travel (?) and building-site adventures, the other notable feature of P7 was the confirmation of my budding genius when I was duly anointed as the Kinloch Primary School Dux.

I do remember that one day, the commonly acknowledged brightest pupils from the two P7 classes, including yours truly, were siphoned off to sit some special tests. I have no recollection of anything that was actually involved in the tests, but I must've done well as it later transpired that the results of these tests were, in fact, to decide on the dux. For anyone unfamiliar with the term, the *Chambers English Dictionary* defines "dux" as "a leader: the top academic prize-winner in a school or class". Shucks! I don't even know if such a title still exists in state schools? Probably not, as it's most likely viewed as representing some form of elitism. I don't agree with elitism at all but there's absolutely nothing wrong with healthy competition, not that any of us explicitly knew we were actually in competition.

Anyway, on the day that I was announced as the winner I casually dropped it into the conversation at lunchtime with Mum. I think she said something like, "Oh, that's good, sonny," while probably not having a Scooby what it meant.

Dad was his usual self on finding out – "Dux, is that because you're quackers?" Ah, that comic talent was wasted – not! Actually, he would proudly trot out that quackers line for years to come – I'll hold back how he described my degrees for later, just to make sure you stick with this tale!

Obviously, they were very proud.

When the official letter came in it specified what I'd won, apart from custody of the engraved silver cup, the Basil Wilson Trophy, for a year, and the prestigious title of school dux – a scholarship to the fee-paying Dundee High School. Dad read this and said, "Do you want to go to Dundee High?"

And, without hesitation, I replied, "No."

See how the decision-making qualities of a natural-born leader manifested themselves so easily?

That whole leader thing is probably in my blood as my middle name, McIntosh, inherited from my mum's family, actually derives from the Gaelic *Mac an Tòisich* and means "son of the leader". So this great achievement was all to be expected really…!

In truth, I probably didn't have a clue what it actually meant, the Dundee High thing, but I did know that I didn't want to be separated from my mates again. I'm also sure I already had some sort of innate working-class distrust of privilege and private education and had no desire to go to a school full of rugby-playing posh kids. Obviously, if I knew then what I know now, it would've been prudent for us all to have given it a bit more serious thought but, on reflection, I'm pretty sure I would've reached exactly the same conclusion, in exactly the same amount of time.

Anyway, why bother with boring old Dundee High School when we were all bound for the brand-new, bright and shiny Carnoustie High…

CHAPTER 5

Joining the big boys

(1971–1973)

So my commute technically increased for the first time ever, but it was still a more than reasonable 0.4 miles, a mere 10-minute stroll across the park which lay about 75 yards from our house, Carnoustie House Grounds. I wasn't getting any better at getting up in the mornings, so making it on time was still always a close-run thing. As with most people, going to secondary school brought about a mixture of excitement, trepidation and downright fear. It's a huge change in a young life going from an environment of the same teacher in the same room all day every day, to moving between rooms every 40 minutes or so and seven or eight teachers altogether. Not to mention all these new people.

Having spent the last seven years with more or less the same cohort – my sabbatical year in Dundee notwithstanding – suddenly we were faced with all these strange people from Monifieth and, worse, from out in the country! I already kind of knew one or two of the Monifieth boys, as we'd played football against them several times over the previous two years, but the whole thing was, I suppose, quite unsettling. Not that anyone would probably have noticed as we pretty much all just got on with it. Maybe the fact that neither the teachers nor our parents made too much of a fuss about it helped us to take it in our stride but, in any event, very soon it was all completely normal.

The organisation of a secondary school demanded that we get accustomed to this strange new entity known as your registration class, supervised by your registration, or regie, teacher, and distinguished by the digit representing your school year followed by the initial letter of your regie teacher's surname. Thus, it came to pass that I was admitted to 1M under the stern gaze of a very, too posh-sounding, elderly English teacher, Mrs Ann Mudie.

Ma Mudie, as she was universally known, was another to fall into the generally hard but fair category, though she was prone to the odd shrieking session if things were somehow going awry. She also happened, through sheer coincidence, to be our English teacher so we did see her quite a lot. She seemed to get quite inordinately excited by a, supposedly, great event that was happening in London in 1972, the opening of the Tutankhamun exhibition. Always one to over-pronounce in a spectacularly plummy tone, Ma really went to town with Tutankhamun – or, TootanHAmoon, with a great breathy run-up to the HAmoon bit!

This whole speaking "wi a bool in her moo" trait was a constant source of amusement for us, especially when she would get all animated over correcting any perceived colloquialisms in our speech.

One day, she unleashed her aforementioned shrieking capabilities on yours truly – "Speak the Queen's English, boy!" which elicited a response of, "She's no my f***ing

Queen!" – inside my young head, not out loud, obviously; I wisnae a daftie wi a death wish!

Another afternoon, I turned up for her English class without my books and jotters. Disaster, but a genuine mistake. For the one and only time in my school career I'd got my days mixed up and brought my Thursday books on a Wednesday, or something similar. Well, she went ballistic.

As I stood there taking her shrieking in my stride I did think, *You're going a wee bit over the top here, are you not?* But she hadn't even started yet.

Having howled herself to a standstill she decided my crime merited a visit to Mr Martin, the Head of English. Spuggie Martin, now he was evil! He appeared to agree that my crime was indeed heinous and decreed that my punishment would be to stand in a corner of his room for an hour, facing the wall behind the door while he taught his class, who universally treated me with sniggering contempt.

One could argue that I did learn my lesson on that occasion, as I never made the same mistake again. Or, one could more correctly have realised that it had been a complete one-off, genuine and relatively trivial error by a truly mortified young boy that was unlikely to ever be made again and that, as an experienced teacher with a duty of pastoral care to her young pupils, one should perhaps be a bit more forgiving! Either way, it never happened again.

At some point during the year Ma acquired a student teacher, Mrs Jones, and she eventually took over as our regie teacher for second year. The only remnant of Ma remaining was her "M" as we graduated to 2M despite technically being 2J. Mrs Jones, Cath, was the archetypal early 1970s dolly bird, all long hair, tight jumpers and short skirts. Very short. She wasn't as much of a yeller, but more reliant on a completely unsmiling death stare, followed by a chillingly delivered piece of sarcasm, should she ever choose to humiliate you for any misdemeanour. But, generally, she was very good, though she was later to provide me with one of the funniest moments of my school career…

Of course, meeting all of these new teachers was a mixed bag. Some were good, actually most of mine were very good, but some weren't so great and one or two were absolutely woeful. It was my good fortune to acquire Mr E. D. Black, or Ed, as my Mathematics teacher. Like Dave Fimister the previous year, here was a man destined to have a great influence on my development. Ed was very stern on the outside, but another really kind and gentle man underneath. And funny. I used to love the way he drew his geometrical diagrams with coloured chalk. Simple things, eh? But they were things of beauty.

I really took to Mathematics. In fact, I pretty much took to everything. I'd always been clever – I was still the reigning dux remember – and interested, and even with new subjects like French and the sciences, nothing much changed. Maybe that was the problem, though it wouldn't fully manifest for a few years, but it was all too easy. I didn't have to work at stuff – it just all came naturally, like it always had. So, when others started to describe me as a swot, I didn't like it one bit. It certainly wasn't given as a compliment, as being labelled a swot was definitely uncool, but I probably got most agitated because it simply wasn't true. In fact, as I would soon find out to my cost, because I'd never had to swot for anything before, when I eventually needed to, I just didn't know how to study properly. Anyway, it didn't happen often, and it was mostly said more or less in jest, and I was strong-minded enough to pretty much shrug it all off and just get on with things.

Which was just as well, as secondary schools were fairly harsh environments back in the 1970s. You didn't want to be showing any weaknesses or otherwise being singled out for attention, or the pack would hunt you down. There were definitely people in every year that you didn't want to cross. Break times were the most dangerous as there was always a chance of something kicking off if one of our resident neds took a dislike to you for whatever reason, or sometimes even just randomly. The trick was to stay away from flashpoints without making it look obvious that was what you were doing, as that alone could merit getting your head kicked in.

This was around the time of the film *A Clockwork Orange*, and everyone was constantly in danger from "a bit of the old ultra-violence". Ridiculously, I was actually able to get in to see the film at our local fleapit, the Pavilion Cinema. A few of us turned up to see this widely publicised and controversial film and when asked if we were over 18 squeaked "Yes" indignantly and were permitted entry without a second glance. We were 12! And no, we weren't early developers.

I loved the film, though even then I hated violence. It was just exciting, to be getting to see something you weren't meant to and that represented a world, however bizarre and repulsive, that your parents just wouldn't get. Even the music, a bit of the old Ludwig Van, seemed exotic. And, of course, the clothes. Bowler hat, Crombie overcoat, braces, white Levi's Sta-Prest trousers rolled up to reveal 10-hole Doc Martens. OK, I'm not going to claim it was a fashion sensation, but there was a certain allure to our impressionable young minds.

One of our acquaintances, a year or two older than us, had the complete outfit and used to parade around of an evening looking like he'd just stepped out of the film. To be brutally honest though, he just looked daft! Not that anyone ever told him of course, as that would've resulted in you being on the receiving end of the old ultra-violence. And before anyone thinks that "getting your head kicked in" was just a turn of phrase, let me assure you that I witnessed it on several occasions though, thankfully, never from the recipient's viewpoint.

Mainly then I managed to avoid trouble. I say mainly as it was literally impossible to avoid everything forever. I did get one smack in the coupon which was completely gratuitous and entirely down to wrong place, wrong person, wrong time, in the cloakrooms one lunchtime. I also acquired a huge gravel-filled hole in my left knee as a result of being pushed over beside the tennis courts on the way out of school.

I seriously can't even remember if that push was accidental, but I do remember the doctor's instructions to get into a bath and scrub the gravel out of the wound with a scrubbing brush. Ouch! Worst of all, that incident ripped a hole in my lovely shiny navy blue Sta-Prest trousers. At least my knee healed up, though I still have the scar – my ultra-cool trousers were mended with a not-quite-so-cool patch by my mum. And there was no question of not wearing them again...

Apart from those minor infractions, the only violence, ultra or otherwise, that I was subjected to was perpetrated by that extreme bunch of sadists – the teachers.

Our woodwork teacher, Mr Fergusson, had a particularly cruel method of maintaining your attention should he feel the need to admonish you for any perceived misdemeanour, minor or otherwise. He would grab a chunk of the hair that we would've optimistically described as sideburns, or sidies – in reality, at this age, it was just the hair hanging down the side of your ear where, one day, sidies might grow! – and pull upwards, literally lifting you off your feet if he was particularly enraged. Ouch!

I only knew one of our peers to have genuine sidies at that time, but they just formed part of what appeared to be a full-body fur coat! We called him Bear, for obvious reasons, and he must've had more testosterone coursing through his hairy body than the rest of us put together! Imagine having to shave more than twice a day, at age 13? And not necessarily just his chin!

Mr Campbell, the music teacher, employed more psychological methods of torture to encourage us to sing, individually or collectively, in front of our peers – he would just scream at you until you finally realised that the embarrassment of revealing your lack of crooning capability was worthwhile in order to, for now at least, shut him up.

There were also many other, some more cunning, tactics employed to keep us recalcitrant youths in order, many of them hangovers from the military system.

Peter Spence was, I believe, a former sergeant major – or something of that order anyway – and he was a wonderful character. Spencie taught Mathematics, but he was also a guidance teacher and had the responsibility of affording pastoral care to those of us newly entered into the junior school, first and second year. He would float magnificently around the corridors resplendent in his gown – think Chic Murray's character in *Gregory's Girl* – looking over the top of the throngs in front of him, and was prone to summon whoever caught his eye with the command, "You, small boy, come here."

If you were ever interrogated by Spencie you were liable to confess to anything just to make the ordeal end – his standard approach was, "I am going to ask you a question to which I already know the answer, so think very carefully before you speak." Genius! He was also a kindly man but, even then, he was one of a dying breed.

And then there was the formal method of punishment that would still be the norm for another decade – the belt. There was a certain status associated with being given the toosh, which on reflection was probably an Angus pronunciation of the tawse, that splendid two- or three-pronged lump of Lochgelly leather that was the ultimate deterrent for schoolchildren of many generations. You didn't want to be getting belted all the time, mainly because it hurt, but also because too much was definitely uncool.

On the other hand, to never get it at all was to be a goody-two-shoes which, in itself, was enough to attract the other kind of violence alluded to earlier. So, for a few years, me and my *droogies* (a hundred thousand appy polly loggies o brother, I will get out of this *Clockwork Orange* mode soon!) maintained a whip chart which detailed the who, when and why and, most importantly, the number of lashes received.

One of the Art teachers, Tom Walker, had a particularly all-encompassing method of administering this form of corporal punishment, combining both mental and physical agony with ritualistic humiliation. Fortunately, I was never to suffer this personally, but I did witness it. He was generally a good guy but, if pushed too far, would completely lose it and, if he decided a belting was the appropriate finale then a process would begin.

First he'd send his victim to stand in a cupboard, with the door half open, facing into the room, with hands up and crossed in the traditional ready-to-receive-the-belt position – the cupboard was in the corner of the room so everyone else could just see his (it was never a girl) paws sticking out beyond the door and, importantly, he couldn't see anybody. Tom would then say, "Before the end of this lesson, you will be belted," and then carry on with the class. If he saw any sign of the hands dropping he would yell, "Get those hands up!" Then, finally, once he decided the moment had arrived, he would silently approach and unleash the full fury of his toosh on his unsuspecting victim's paws – ouch!

My most painful experience resulted from being put out of the room by the most pathetic female teacher we'd ever experienced – honestly, you'd have to have seen this woman in action to believe it. When even pre-adolescent girls refer to you as "Nae Tits", you should know you've got credibility issues!

She taught a minority, archaic and totally pointless subject – Classics, if you're wondering – that, for some unknown reason, was compulsory for our first two years, and she had the charisma and classroom control of a house brick. Actually, a house brick was more threatening as you could injure yourself on it, and it was infinitely more useful to civilisation. Words fail me, even today.

When she finally totally lost control, as she eventually would in every class, every day, her only tactic was to put someone out in the corridor. The other teachers knew this so, if the particularly evil ones were bored at any time during the day, and fancied inflicting a bit of pain, they would go for a walk round the corridors and make sure to pass her door. On the day that I was randomly ejected it was my misfortune that it was one of the hardest of that particular breed who happened upon me.

Using the "you must've done something wrong" mentality prevalent of the day, he took me down to his office and executed two belters, pun entirely intended. Duly chastened, he sent me back up and, on the way, I decided to visit the toilet and experiment with the therapeutic effects of cold running water on my pulsating palms. It helped, a little. This must've taken me all of five minutes but, on my way back to the classroom, who did I bump into? Yep!

"Where have you been, boy?" he demanded.

"I went to the toilet, sir," I offered meekly.

"Well, you've obviously not learned your lesson then, follow me…"

So we trooped back down to his lair where he delivered another two mighty blows to my already numbed, or so I thought, paws. The earlier target practice had obviously warmed him up even more than my hands, as this time he crashed his tawse down at what seemed like at least double the ferocity of five minutes earlier.

"Now, you'll go straight back this time…"

Too right, I wasn't risking another two!

Still, perversely, all's well that ends well. I got almighty kudos for taking four of the best from one of the meanest dudes in town, and my teacher at least had the good grace to look shamefaced for being responsible for this outstanding act of barbarity. Not that I could write for the rest of the day, mind…

This period also saw the beginning of a growing awareness of girls. Now, obviously, they'd always been around, but had always previously seemed pretty much just a bit of an annoyance. Now they suddenly seemed, well, pretty. I suppose there'd been a couple of flirtations when we were way too young and stupid to know that we were interested, or indeed what we were interested in and why. The occasional game of Kiss, Cuddle or Torture in the dim and distant past had only proved their annoying qualities really. Especially when the kiss and/or cuddle that the girls were seeking was actually the torture for us boys anyway. But mainly, they appeared to be just silly little things that existed in their own wee worlds and didn't encroach on football or any of the daftness that occupied us boys.

Now, suddenly and almost without warning, our hormones were flourishing and their appeal was starting to grow even if we didn't fully understand why. They started changing shape too, as did we, but at least our changes were kept well under wraps – theirs were blooming out all over!

I'd noticed one wee girl in our first few weeks there. She was from Monifieth, therefore exotic by definition, and she was a good athlete and hockey player. Not that anything was going to happen by the way – I was much too shy for any of that – but it's worth noting when this infatuation started in case it crops up again later. Well, obviously it is going to crop up again later or I wouldn't be mentioning it!

If that was a specific example then there were other more general cases on a daily basis, and the whole subject of girls began to form part of our everyday interest and conversation. Some of our more outgoing peers even started going out (did you see what I did there?) and coming back with tales of bravado that only served to (a) intensify our interest, and (b) make us even more terrified and reluctant!

Talking of terrified, we were also introduced to the Carnoustie ritual – I don't know if it happened in all schools? – of the entire PE curriculum being taken over each December by Scottish country dancing. What? Every PE lesson would involve the entire year group being herded into the games hall with the boys lined up against one wall and the girls lined up on the opposite wall. All of the PE teachers would be in attendance and one of them was in charge of the one small record player, which was absolutely dwarfed by the size of the hall. The teachers would then demonstrate whatever dance it was that we were going to be learning – Dashing White Sergeant, Eightsome Reel, Canadian (?) Barn Dance, Waltz, Strip the Willow or, my personal favourite (not – for obvious reasons!) the Gay Gordons. Then came the evil part, as the boys (usually) were instructed to cross the hall and choose your partners – surely there's some human rights violation here?

Our games hall was big, probably some 25 yards wide. That means a long, long walk towards... what? Or, more appropriately, who? Unless you were already in a relationship, which few of us were, who were you going to pick? You couldn't pick someone you actually fancied, as that would be too much of a public confession and ran the risk of rejection in front of the entire year. On the other hand, whoever you did choose would mean that you would be immediately accused of fancying them whether you actually did or not. Yet you didn't want to get landed with whoever was left over, so you had to do something!

Maybe because we were all in the same boat we somehow managed to do whatever we had to do, all the while affecting a general air of disinterest in a vain attempt to mask our outright embarrassment. Then, the dancing would begin. This was when we all realised that choosing your partner was only the start – now you actually had to touch each other!

Anyway, none of us had any choice so one way or another we got on with it and, with the wee record player straining at maximum volume to distortedly fill the cavernous hall, Willie Simmons – yes, I told you he'd make a reappearance! – would be striding around shouting out the instructions, "Forward, two, three, hop, backward, two, three, hop, side skip, clap, side skip, clap, back together and…" Or words to that effect.

Each and every one of us just wanted it all to be over. The only thing that would prove to be even more embarrassing would be that, on the final day, one of the younger teachers would put on some pop record and say, "Now, do your own dance," and exacerbate the cringe by dancing with one of the other teachers. In front of us! It's no easy being an adolescent!

And, by the way, none of this should be viewed as in any way misogynistic – I'm acutely aware, and was even back then, of how difficult it must've been for the girls having to stand there passively as they watched the uncouth hordes lumbering across the hall, experiencing exactly the same emotions about partner choice yet having no say in the matter. The only meagre attempt to even things up was that, once or twice during the month, it was them that were instructed to choose one of us… yikes!

We had two other major events in that very same torture chamber of a games hall in that first year. The first was the official opening of the school, a grand event with the entire school seated in the hall along with the great and the good of Carnoustie society to witness Princess Alexandra perform the ribbon-cutting ceremony. I assume there was the cutting of a ribbon but, as you might expect given my innate anti-monarchy leanings, I wasn't paying attention to any of that malarkey – I was just hoping hard that she wouldn't stop and try to speak to me as I was quite near the end of a row that she walked past.

The other event was the first, and I think only, school Christmas Fair held on a December Saturday. There were stalls, homebaking (courtesy of the Home Economics classes and staff), "artisan" trinkets (courtesy of the Woodwork and Metalwork classes and staff) and various other demonstrations and games, like the Physics teachers supervising one of those buzz wire games or the PE teachers setting up some skill tests. They had one in the gym upstairs that involved trying to chip a football through a hoop around ten yards away – after I'd scored three times out of three attempts I was chased away by the supervising sixth-year pupil! The whole thing was "in aid of school funds", though what use those funds were put to was never made obvious to us.

Football and music continued to be my main interests throughout this time, when not thinking about girls obviously, but also my bike. On Christmas Day 1971, I became the proud owner of a gold and green racing bike. I'd like to think my parents had learned from their previous traumatisation of their son through offering choices, but how they managed to keep this complete surprise under wraps until Christmas Day itself is beyond me. It probably helped that Dad had kept the bike in a friend's garage along the street and only retrieved it after I'd gone to bed on Christmas Eve.

I couldn't wait to try it out and so, before lunchtime, I sped off on my new trusty steed resplendent, also wearing my spanking new Gola Harrier trainers. White, red stripe, suede toecap, the epitome of cool. Or as cool as you could get from the *Kays Catalogue* at least.

My brother, his wife and his daughter Gail were coming to us for Christmas dinner and, after a few laps of our street, I headed off to meet them on the way, and to show off the new bike of course. I had all kinds of plans for it. I would get a water bottle, and some flags for the handlebars, and badges on the frame. I never actually did any of that, except for one badge, Dundee United of course, on the mudguard.

For a while I took it to school where we all, trustingly, left our machines untethered in the bike shed. Surprisingly few ever went missing, but I soon reverted to walking to school again as I missed the companionship of my mates. Or I got fed up, whatever.

That bike served me well over the years, and my brother too. When he later went self-employed, he pressed my bike into service as his work vehicle, not that he bothered with mere details like asking my permission. Naturally he was confined to working in Carnoustie because of the obvious limitations of two-wheeled self-propelled transportation, but I had a job getting the bike back. I've still got it, at the back of my shed, though I seriously doubt it'll be roadworthy!

My football activities consisted of playing for the school team and watching United with Dad. Around this time, a few of the lads had started going to the matches on their own but, thankfully, I never did. I'm glad to say I always enjoyed going with Dad and, as we did that uninterrupted for over 50 years, he clearly reciprocated that feeling. It was just a great father–son thing to do, and I really do treasure the memories.

Playing was strange in that period though. I always got selected in the team of at least the year above, so when my friends were playing U13, I was playing U14 or U15, and when they moved to U14, I was playing U15 or U18. That meant I was always in a team with boys a year or more older than me. I didn't really enjoy that aspect, as it was another potential bullying situation. Not that I was ever bullied, but I just wasn't one of them. Still, what doesn't kill you makes you stronger, as the cliché goes, and I suppose it did me no harm in the long run.

Some of my friends also started playing in the Sunday Boys' League at this time, mainly for Monifieth Tayside. I never fancied it for some reason, probably still too shy to put myself out there, though I did flirt with it briefly later on.

Two games we played – both in Kirriemuir so presumably one in first year, the other in second year – stick in my mind.

The first one involved us wearing, for the first time, the brand new red and black vertical striped nylon football shirts. Now, one of the advantages being touted of nylon kit at the time was that it didn't retain moisture in the same way as old-fashioned cotton did… That game in Kirrie was played in an absolute downpour and those state-of-the-art-shirts just got heavier and heavier, stretching longer and longer, until it was virtually impossible for us drookit wee laddies to move, never mind play football! The bus journey home was interesting too, with the steam from around 50 rapidly drying out but half-drowned youths filling the air!

The second game brings back more painful memories… Kirrie had a free kick not far outside our penalty box, and

I was marking somebody a few yards to the right of our defensive wall. When the Kirrie boy hit his free kick directly at goal, the ball cannoned off the hip of the furthest right player in our wall and planted itself directly, squarely and unexpectedly in my groin with no opportunity to react before it struck its painful blow – ouch! I think that was my first experience of that sickening pain, though, as all footballers will understand, it was never likely to be the last.

Still, I should count my blessings because on the one and only occasion that I was unable to avoid playing rugby, it was someone else who was to suffer far more than I in the same anatomical region. Our PE teacher warned all of us football guys one day that we were going to play rugby and that we were going to try and play it properly, not just turn it into a game of football – he made it quite clear there would be dire consequences if we didn't comply. He also said that he didn't want to see any of us feigning injury to try and get out of it that way, stating, "If I see any of you lying on the ground complaining of injury then I fully expect to have to call an ambulance."

At the end of the game there was indeed one poor soul lying on the ground, and he did have to call that ambulance! We were able to watch the ambulance making its way across the pitch, from the window of our next class, and transport our unfortunate comrade off to hospital where he would have his testicle stitched back into place! There but for the grace...

My awareness of football beyond our shores was increasing rapidly, probably initiated by the previous year's World Cup in Mexico being the first major televised event I'd witnessed, and also in colour. The advent of that wonderful football magazine *Shoot* also played a part, and through that

I not only learned much more about Manchester United and George Best, but also discovered Johan Cruyff and Ajax Amsterdam as well as being reacquainted with Barcelona. Each magazine would be scrutinised first for any mention of Dundee United, then re-examined for photos which could help decorate my bedroom.

I was sent away one weekend, I've no idea where and that kind of thing just never happened, but I was sent away. In my absence, Dad entirely redecorated my bedroom – two tangerine walls, white ceiling and… one black wall.

Now, hang on, the important point here isn't that I lived in a three-walled room – no, the other wall just happened to be wood-panelled. A black wall? Nowadays, you can buy tartan paint if that's what you want, maybe, but back then the only way to get a black wall was to use blackboard paint. Which came in very small cans because, well, how much paint do you need for a blackboard? A lot less than you need for a whole wall, let me tell you. So, several small cans of blackboard paint later I had a wholly unique and magnificent black wall. Class. And the envy of my friends, even those who didn't share my football affiliations, for years.

Finally, but wonderfully, the *pièce de résistance*… in the middle of the black wall, a giant poster of my hero, George Best. Now, with hindsight, there was something potentially homoerotic about this as George was topless in the photo but I can honestly say that never entered my mind. In 1972, George retired and headed off to Marbella, and I think that poster must've come from round about that time.

I loved my new room. Not that it encouraged me to keep it tidy though. To my mother's eternal despair, my room always looked like a bombsite. Left to my own devices, our whole house would probably still look like that today, as my wife likes to remind me.

Not only did I have a magnificent tangerine-and-black bedroom, but I also had my own living room, complete with stereo and TV, upstairs. Our entire upper floor had been converted into a room by our modernist architect predecessor, albeit a very long, skinny room which peaked at around five and a half feet in height at the apex. It wouldn't, indeed doesn't, satisfy building regulations to be described as a bona fide room nowadays, but it was a great den, and again, much envied by my friends. I used to spend hours up there alone listening to my growing music collection at quite extreme volumes.

Apart from the Beatles, I'd adopted the glam-rockers Sweet and the art-rock band 10cc as my particular favourites. Sweet was a classic example of me going against trend and being quite individual in my tastes. Most of my peers dismissed them as a pretty-boy, probably gay, bubblegum pop band whereas I was fully invested in the hard-rocking self-compositions initially only featuring on the B-sides of their singles. It's fair to say I was the only Sweet fan I knew, but I viewed that positively.

I'd also pick up random singles depending on whatever took my fancy, but we generally didn't have oodles of spare cash floating around for frivolous purchases, so every record bought was carefully researched and sought out.

Other things I bought during this period included "Hold Your Head Up" by Argent, "Woodstock" by Matthews Southern Comfort and "I Am... I Said" by Neil Diamond. Now, once again with the benefit of hindsight, that's a fairly eclectic mix.

In 1973, school life would suddenly take on a much more serious meaning and, just like the Christmas tree and stereo/

golf clubs debacle of earlier years, the element of choice involved was enough to hang a dark cloud over my young head for a wee while. Yes, the bane of every Scottish 14-year-old's life arrives during the second half of your second year – the Options Form. Basically, this involved the selection of courses that you intended to follow for the next two years leading towards O grade certification. But it wasn't an entirely open choice.

Because of timetabling restrictions, if you wanted to do Geography you couldn't do History as well because both of those subjects were in the same column, or you could do both if you selected History from another column, but then that ruled out doing Chemistry. Or something like that. Obviously I'm making up the detail but, hopefully, you get the picture, and you probably went through something similar yourself.

Anyway, I don't recall my choice being too complicated as I was good at everything. Mathematics, Arithmetic and English were compulsory, I liked Geography, I needed a foreign language so French was in, I wanted to do Chemistry and Physics so Biology fell off the end but, no matter, I could pick that up later in fifth year. Or at least that was the advice of the day and, crucially, that particular bit of misinformation would cost two of my friends their dreams of studying medicine at university when they were told, belatedly and on the point of application three years hence, that they required A passes at Higher in all three sciences in the one sitting. Thankfully, one of them did eventually make it as a GP but his first degree only exempted him from the first year of his self-funded medical degree, and he finally got there only after around ten years of study!

No such forward planning for me though as, at this stage, I had no clue what I wanted to do. To be honest, I still don't! Well, that's not exactly true, as I wanted to play professional football. And, to be honest again, I still do! But that was not quite the career choice you can plan for, at least not in them days. So, the die was cast and once I'd overcome, temporarily, the trauma of thinking about what I wanted to do and made the choices for the next two years, it was time to leave junior school behind and move on up amongst the big boys in middle school. And girls...

CHAPTER 6

Stuck in the middle

(1973–1975)

It was all change again then as we were all gathered into the games hall on the first morning back to be allocated to our new registration classes. The process involved us all sitting randomly on the floor then, whenever our name was called, getting up and walking to wherever your allocated teacher was standing.

Now, getting up and doing anything in the full gaze of your peers is never a comfortable time, even more so when you're 14 years old, but some definitely suffered more than most. The formality of the times was evident in the mode of calling the names – very strictly your surname followed by your first initial. And so it came to pass that an entire year group fell about in hysterics when a very quiet little girl was summoned by her absolutely innocent surname but unfortunate, to our ears, first initial – "Green, P."!

Anyway, a little later, to no notable reaction, Craigie, G. was duly inducted into 3P and came under the watchful eye of Mr Patterson, or Techie Eckie as he was affectionately nicknamed in a way that also distinguished him from the other Alec Patterson, the fearsome Head of Art.

The funny thing is, all these men I thought of as fearsome, evil or hard as nails, and all the women I thought of as stern, straight-laced and humourless, when I was destined to return as a colleague some 12 years later, their veils were lifted and each of these hitherto unsmiling, apparently fascistic personas revealed themselves to be warm, funny and genuinely engaging human beings. Well, most of them!

What I was to discover all those years later was that most of them, as people, were quite the opposite of the teacher that they presented as, and that most of teaching is actually an act. Techie Eckie adopted the eminently sensible idea of working with what he had rather than trying to mould what was clearly never going to fit.

Stooge and I used to arrive at school each morning at the extreme upper end of on time and some, probably most, regie teachers would have considered it to be, in fact, late. But we were, at least, consistent, and so Eckie, quite early in our relationship, decided that he wouldn't send his registration slip round to the school office, where the formal attendances would be recorded, until we'd shown our faces. This worked on the basis that no one was likely to arrive after us, and if they did then they *were* late!

Away from school, this would be the year that, like all boys of my age, I got carried along by the prospect of the Scottish national team playing at the World Cup finals for the first time in our history, in West Germany. It was a huge event when we beat Czechoslovakia at Hampden to qualify, and the build-up of excitement started immediately afterwards.

But even more exciting for me was that, before those World Cup finals even began, we had the not-at-all-insignificant fact that my beloved Dundee United reached the Scottish Cup

Final for the first time in their history. Well, it was actually the second time, but the first doesn't apparently officially count as it was in 1940 during wartime, and designated as the Scottish War Emergency Cup Final – don't mention the war – and, according to my dad and various neutral reports I've researched, United were cheated out of a result (not for the last time!) by Rangers – *plus ça change, plus c'est la même chose*!

Anyway... this was a huge event as in my lifetime we'd never even reached a semi-final before. We were drawn to play against Hearts in the semi, at Hampden, but my dad said we couldn't go because he had some work thing that he couldn't get out of. Well, this prompted a depth of despair never before seen in young Gordie, and my continued bleating had the desired effect when he eventually agreed, only a few days before the game, that I could go as long as Tommy agreed to accompany me on a supporter's bus. Thankfully, thankfully, he did agree so we set off excitedly on 6 April 1974 on what was, for me, a huge adventure, only to witness a poor game in a terrible stadium which resulted in a lacklustre 1–1 draw.

I remember walking back to our bus and being shielded by Tommy as Hearts-supporting hooligans pelted the United buses with rocks, breaking several windows, though, thankfully, not ours.

On the way back, we stopped somewhere to invade a chip shop, and I remember the bus doing what seemed like a 65-point turn in order to extricate itself from a one-way street!

The other notable feature of that day was that evening brought the Swedish pop phenomenon ABBA into everyone's lives when they won the Eurovision Song Contest with "Waterloo".

Anyway, a mere three days later "the history books on the shelves" would be recording that United trounced Hearts 4–2 in the replay, also at Hampden, but no amount of pleading persuaded Dad that we should go to that game. Only in confirming some of the details while writing this have I discovered that the replay was held on my 15th birthday – a very happy birthday indeed!

Of course, that meant we had our first real Scottish Cup Final to look forward to, against Celtic. Although they appeared invincible at the time, and were en route to their first nine in a row league title record, I was confident – I always was! We had the young Andy Gray, "the leader o the team, the finest centre forward that the world has ever seen", as well as other up and coming future legends, Dave Narey and Graeme Payne. Alongside seasoned veterans Doug Smith, Archie Knox, George Fleming and others, I reckoned we had a good chance. And hadn't we been the only team to beat Celtic domestically, twice, back in 1967 when they won the European Cup? Exciting times.

Alas, those very same history books will record that we lost 0–3, though the game was by no means as one-sided as that outcome paints it. We had driven through to the game – me, Dad, Tommy, my schoolfriend John and my younger cousin Scott. Scott neglected to tell us until after the game that he was, in fact, a Celtic supporter – the wide smile which accompanied this revelation soon disappeared as Tommy threatened to throw his Celtic scarf, which he'd carefully kept hidden, out of the window if he opened his mouth again before we got home! He would've too!

On reflection, the month of April in 1974 was a really significant one for young Gordon. Apart from all of that football-related excitement, there was also the eagerly awaited, by me anyway, launch of the first proper album by my musical heroes, Sweet. I say proper because their only previous album had been a greatest hits collection of early singles and B-sides, *Funny How Sweet Coco Can Be*. But *Sweet Fanny Adams* was to be the first time that the majority of the tracks would be band compositions, and therefore much more reflective of their hard-rocking B-sides that had got me thoroughly hooked on their sound in the first place.

I just had to get this album at the first available opportunity, so I persuaded Dad to detour into the centre of Dundee, after a United home game on the Saturday, in order to make it to Bruce's record store in Reform Street before closing time. We made it, I bought it, and... I was excited.

After tea I retreated to my upstairs room and scrutinised the cover in detail before carefully, lovingly, placing the 12-inch slab of vinyl on the turntable. Then... well, I was blown away. I can genuinely still remember how I felt when the opening riffs of "Set Me Free" came blasting out of my Rigonda speakers. Wow, just wow! Then the glorious harmonies of "Heartbreak Today", with the little pause before the short instrumental break at the end. "No You Don't", "Rebel Rouser" and "Peppermint Twist" completed side one – life before CDs, eh? – before I was compelled to move to turn over and discover the delights of side two.

People always say "the first time's the best" in a whole range of contexts, and with this as my evidence, I'd have to agree. Absolutely brilliant and, for me, sounds as fresh today as it did then. It's one of my very few regrets that I never had the opportunity to see the classic Sweet line-up play live, though I have seen Andy Scott's modern-day version a couple of times – excellent though they are, it would've been fantastic to see the originals at their peak...

This 1973–75 period wasn't a particularly good one for me overall in terms of my introduction, or not as it turned out, to the live music experience. While most of my friends were doing everything they could to secure tickets to see Bowie, in 1973, and Wings, in 1975, at the Caird Hall, young Gordie inexplicably decided to catch them next time... there never was a next time in Dundee for either of those legends!

Having, apparently, learned from those errors of judgement I did, however, make sure that I had a ticket to see one of my other favourite bands, 10cc, and was really excited about finally going to my first gig. Unfortunately fate, or more precisely the Dundee Council electricians, conspired against me and the concert was cancelled at the last minute because the sparkies went on strike!

Having said that, the first concert I did manage to get to later that year was pretty memorable – Queen, while "Bohemian Rhapsody" was in the middle of its nine-week, chart-topping run! Ever the cynic though, I distinctly remember being distinctly unimpressed when Freddie Mercury took to the stage shouting, "Good evening, Dundee," while throwing red roses into the crowd – spectacular as it appeared, I just thought, *You've no idea where Dundee even is – somebody just tells you the relevant name every night.* Still think I'm right about that, by the way...

Back to school – third year was when all things academic suddenly started to appear quite serious. Any time there was any carrying on or missed homework or whatever, most of the teachers would trot out some dire warning about how important the O grade exams were and how little time we had to prepare. Little time? Two years!

Nowadays, with the benefits of hindsight, experience and maturity, I'd agree with that sentiment. But when you're young there's some kind of inverse dog-years timing process going on, and two years is an awfully long time away.

Anyway, everything appeared to be moving along relatively seamlessly. I was fortunate enough to retain the stewardship of Uncle Ed as my Mathematics guru, and the familiar faces of Cath Jones in English, Bill Anderson in Geography and Jim "Mushki" Ritchie in Physics. I feel comfortable using their first names now, mainly as they were all later to become colleagues, indeed friends. Although I don't think Jim's nickname was ever properly explained to him, even later on – it was probably because he drove a Russian car, a Moskvich, at the time – a bit like a Lada or a Skoda – and we all thought he looked a bit Russian as well (?) so, somehow, in our adolescent minds, Mushki seemed appropriate? Maybe you had to be there.

Another theory is that his toothy expression made him look a bit like Muskie the muskrat from the *Deputy Dawg* cartoon! Either way, Mushki was better than his alternative nickname, Mabasa… just run that into his surname for another example of classic Scottish schoolboy humour!

Anyway, one day Jim got a phone call from the school office while he was teaching – an unusual occurrence – and he immediately rushed off to meet a breakdown lorry which had unexpectedly arrived to tow his car away. But there was nothing wrong with his car and he hadn't ordered a breakdown lorry. Somebody had phoned the local garage pretending to be Jim and told them his car had broken down and could they take it away please? To the best of my knowledge nobody, least of all Jim, ever found out who the prankster had been.

In other science-related news, Chemistry became an altogether more attractive prospect as our new teacher, Mrs Masson, was extremely easy on the eye (I did mention earlier that hormonal changes were afoot!). If all of this was, so far, all good and comforting, most of that feeling was about to be undone by the introduction of our new French teacher, Miss Doig...

Now, most people have some redeeming qualities, no matter how unpleasant they may seem at times. And, again with the benefit of the aforementioned hindsight, maturity and a smattering of wisdom, we only ever see snapshots of our teachers as human beings while we are at school. Yes, the good ones do let their personalities shine through to some extent, but they still have to balance that out with the act that maintains discipline, order and progress amongst a bunch of, often, bone idle, disinterested, over-excitable teenagers. Having said all that, what about Miss Doig?

Let's start with the facts. The class she was entrusted with was the top set of third-year O grade French candidates. In my case, I had achieved marks in the 90s during first and second year under Mr Simpson's guidance, and I was generally considered to be pretty good at French. In fact, I was what is commonly referred to now, thanks to the influence of Americana on our culture, a straight A student. And most of my third-year French classmates fell into that category too. But our collective performances during that fateful year fell faster than a Lehman Brothers balance sheet.

Now, it would be unkind to suggest the woman was technically mad, or whatever alternative more politically correct diagnosis as may be deemed more acceptable nowadays, and I have no medical expertise to justify such an assertion anyway, but there was definitely something wrong with her. She made stern into an art form. She dressed like a relic from some 1950s black-and-white film in her muddy green and brown tweeds – I know you can't distinguish green and brown, muddy or otherwise, in a black-and-white film but allow me some artistic interpretation here. Her greying hair was swept tightly back into a bun and she had unforgiving spectacles perched on the end of her nose.

We were not allowed to talk, which is a little disconcerting, not to say self-defeating, in a language class, and minor offences like forgetting a pencil were punishable by death. Almost. Unlike today, where children appear far too keen to assert their rights and parents, too, appear generally to take their side whatever the truth, she was the only teacher that I ever complained about seriously to my parents.

As it turned out, I wasn't the only one and, when my dad happened to meet up with a friend's father, somehow her name cropped up and they discovered that, completely independently, they were both getting the same story. Similar discussions were happening between other parents and eventually some of them decided that something should be done. I know it was the only time my dad ever visited the school, outwith a formal parents' evening, to find out what was really going on and express concern over a situation, and it turned out he wasn't the only one.

What happened next remains a wee bit of a mystery, but legend has it that one day she was summoned to the Headmaster's office, but presumably knowing what was coming, she never arrived – she simply walked out of school, drove home and never returned. What I do know for a fact was that sometime in the middle of that term she did disappear, never to be seen again. Unfortunately, the damage by that time had been done and our class of high-flying, top-scoring Francophiles had been turned into a collective of serial exam failures and, basically, in the course of one school year the top set had effectively become the bottom set. Some achievement, for which we should salute you, Miss Doig, but only with one finger!

Other than that not-exactly-minor hiccup, third year passed without any truly memorable events. I was still a straight A (*moins la langue française*) student and life was pretty much rolling nicely along. Yet if third year had contained many dire warnings about the importance and proximity of the looming O grade exams, in fourth year our teachers took it to a whole new level.

In our youthful minds everything was still a whole year away, or seven doggy/teenager years, but as I was to realise much later on, a school year is not really a year. Generally, we go back to school around the end of the second week in August for roughly six uninterrupted weeks, and then break for what is now known as the October holiday – back in the day, this was affectionately, universally and, I think, technically even, known as the Tattie Holidays. Or the Tatties. Two weeks off to pay homage to our agrarian roots, before returning to school for around ten weeks leading up to Christmas. Another two weeks off for the festive festivities then back in for the long, dark haul through January, February and March to Easter. Or the Easter holidays at any rate, which tend to bear no relation whatsoever to the actual positioning of that movable Christian feast.

Anyway, in the years that contain formal exams, that's about your lot, as after that two-week break you're pretty much right into it. So, let me make a quick calculation here... 1 school year (= 7 doggy/teenager years) = 30 weeks, approximately. Take a school day as 6 hours, multiply by 5 days a week × 30 weeks and we've got 900 hours, or around 37.5 days – just over a month... hmm, maybe we should've listened to the warnings!

Arthur Simpson was the experienced hand parachuted in to attempt to rescue our failing French class in fourth year. He was old-school so, although he was extremely kind and encouraging, he could also go off on one if he thought you weren't pulling your weight. He'd taught me in first year, and I well remember the day a new pupil arrived in our class and Arthur's hilarious attempts to get him to say "a cup of tea" – "*une tasse de thé*" – in French. The fact that the boy was Chinese, had just arrived from China and didn't have a word of English didn't deter the bold Arthur from smilingly encouragingly at him to participate in the lesson!

Despite his best efforts, including providing after school twilight classes, Arthur was definitely pushing uphill with most of us. One day, when handing back our homework, he took umbrage at the cover of my jotter, onto which I'd inscribed the words *Desolation Boulevard*, the title of Sweet's second album. Unfortunately, Arthur was neither cognisant of, nor interested in, pop trivia and he took the words literally, informing me in excruciatingly harsh detail that the contents of my jotter were indeed desolate!

Looking back now, it surprises me how little of the actual in-school stuff from third and fourth year, August 1973 to June 1975, has stayed with me. It's almost as if they represented holding years or some transitional period between being a wee boy and becoming a young man. Maybe that's why it's called middle school?

Even out of school, despite the obvious, and inevitable, hormonal activity resulting in increasing interest in the female population, there really was nothing much to specifically get excited about over this two-year period. We'd all started to frequent discos held, mainly, in church halls in both Carnoustie and Monifieth, yet actually dancing with a girl was still a relatively rare occurrence. I was still keeping my eye, from a distance, on the girl I'd fancied since the first weeks of first year but, well, it's always best not to rush these things. I did develop a wee obsession with another girl for a short period, but she wasn't backward in coming forward and averted any potential movement by confiding in me one day that she liked me, but she would only ever go out with boys who were in gangs. Each to their own!

The only misdemeanours that I was ever involved in didn't involve physical violence or vandalism – though I'm sure a whole range of unfortunate homeowners would disagree with the second of those while quite keen to inflict the first as revenge – as each autumn we would happily roam the streets of Carnoustie upholding that fine Scottish tradition, dobbing. Yes, the dobbing season only lasted a few weeks but, in the days before the five-a-day recommendations, it was our way of topping up our fruit intake for the year by "helping" with the domestic harvest! OK, it was downright theft – let's be honest – but that never occurred to our teenage minds; we just viewed it as a form of sport and relished pitting our wits against those unsuspecting residents that had the best apple, pear and plum trees.

One fine evening, three of us were spotted while surveying the fruit-yielding potential of the garden of a large house in Maule Street, so we scarpered quickly, running along the road for a bit before turning into Green Lane where we felt we were out of both range and sight and, therefore, safe. As we giggled away while recovering our breath, we turned around to see a police car turn into the lane and come towards us – "F★★★, act casual lads."

They pulled up alongside, wound the window down and, eyeing us suspiciously, said, "Aye, aye, boys, what are you up to tonight?"

"Nothing much, officers," is what I remember our response to be.

"So why were you running just now?" was the obvious follow-up question, to which we nervously offered, "Eh, just a wee bit of exercise…"

They looked a little unconvinced at this, so out came the notebooks, "Aye, well, we'll just take a wee note of your names, just in case we hear of anything later on."

I can't remember whether they looked at me or Stooge first, but I can still see and hear what happened after we'd given our names and they turned to the third leg of our teenage trio.

"Clifford Appleton," he said confidently – well, he would, because that was his name!

Both of them looked up from their notebooks and screwed their eyes up as they stared at Cliff before one of them said, "Are you taking the piss, son?"

As Cliff protested his innocence both Stooge and I were absolutely bursting to laugh out loud but had to hold it in until they got back into their car and drove off. Priceless!

Cliff, or Cliffy, as he preposterously preferred to be called – we never did! – was also the only person I ever knew to choose pre-recorded cassette tapes as his primary source of musical entertainment over vinyl LPs, and he could never be convinced that this was an unwise choice on many grounds. Now, in the digital era, I can't see there ever being a cassette revival to mirror that of vinyl!

Yet in many ways, fourth year would mark a rite of passage for the young Gordon. Or several actually. Not only did I turn 16 right before this important diet of exams – funny turn of phrase that, diet of exams – but those exams definitely marked the beginning of the end of my age of academic innocence. It turned out to be the last time that I'd get away without really trying, though I still wouldn't realise that until much, much later on. Well, you wouldn't, would you?

I really enjoyed the exams. The whole study leave idea where, for a whole month, you only turned up at school if you had an exam, was a revelation. Long lies during term time – pick it out! Even on exam days, nothing started at 9 a.m., so there were still technically long lies to be enjoyed, and some exams didn't even start until the afternoon – bonus! And nothing lasted up to 4 p.m. so, again, even exam days involved early finishes.

If this description gives the impression that my sole interest in going to school around this time involved how much time I could spend away from school, then that's thoroughly accurate. I was never a kid who hated school, but that didn't mean that the alternative wasn't preferable. And long lies were always good – it's an adolescent thing. Funny how I would struggle to be up in time for school Monday through Friday and yet, come Saturday morning, I would leap out of bed at whatever ungodly hour necessary to fit in with the travel arrangements of the school football team. In that respect, once again, I do not claim to be unique, but it's an interesting observation on the mindset and body clocks of teenagers.

After all the exams were over and the study leave finally came to an end, we then returned to school in dribs and drabs to go through the dreaded Options and Choices routine all over again. Cue more completely irrational agonising and sleepless nights for *moi*. Yep, that whole indecisive "am I doing the right thing?" thing kicked in again.

This time, due to the demands of Highers, there were only five columns to choose from and nothing was compulsory. I had proved my straight A status in the exams (*moins la langue française*, which ended up in a desultory D grade – cheers again, Miss Doig!), so I had a completely free choice for my Highers, and actually had teachers competing over me. That was interesting, if unexpected, but only served to increase my feelings of pressure over the choice.

In the end, it actually proved to be quite straightforward. Mathematics and English, though no longer compulsory, were a given, as were Physics and Chemistry as they were logical choices for a straight A boy of sound rational mind. My choice then lay between Higher Geography, which Bill Anderson was especially keen I should do, or O grade Biology. Remember, we couldn't do the three sciences in one year due to the serious flaw in our school's timetabling policy, so this was year one of catch-up with the intention of doing Higher Biology in sixth year therefore ending up with all three sciences at Higher.

Having to tell Bill that I was doing O grade Biology in preference to the Higher in his subject was agony – I really felt I was letting him down. Still, that was the decision and once done it was, unusually, quickly forgotten and my agonies subsided, for a while.

The other big decision I made was not to repeat O grade French, and this was a biggie as a foreign language was a fundamental requirement for entry to any course at university and, as was becoming increasingly clear, that was where I was undoubtedly headed. To do what exactly was still to be decided, at an emotional cost on a scale not yet encountered, but I was inexorably headed for the hallowed halls. Excellent alliteration there, even though I do say it myself.

As the end-of-term feeling escalated, and we were all clearly feeling demob happy, an opportunity for what we thought was innocent mischief presented itself. One of our peers was leaving, having only joined us that year – after exhausting the patience of his private residential school – to retake his exams. On his final day, at morning interval, a group of us dragged him, not quite kicking and screaming, and threw him into the ornamental pond in the middle of the school quadrangle. We actually thought we had been very considerate, taking his watch off first to keep it safe, and we also thought nobody would notice – despite the fact that the pond was directly overlooked by the teachers' staffroom!

Anyway, we all returned to our classes, including the thoroughly drookit victim, feeling mightily pleased with ourselves. But about ten minutes into our first lesson, the door opened and there was the redoubtable Ed Black fixing his eyes directly on *petit moi* – "Right, Craigie, and your little chums, come with me." Hmm, this wasn't good but, as I embarrassedly followed him into the corridor, I was utterly astonished to realise that another three or four of my "little chums" had accepted their fate and had volunteered to fess up too!

Now, despite the fact that I really liked Ed, and that he'd always been kind with me, this was all a bit squeaky bum time as he also had a reputation as one of the hard hitters, literally, when it came to corporal punishment. Anyway, we all trooped shamefacedly down to his office whereupon Ed informed us that our erstwhile victim had already been sent home – he'd simply followed the trail of water to extricate him from his class! He told us what a foolish act it had been, that the boy could've caught anything from the stagnant water in that pool, and that we'd almost given old Mrs Batchelor a heart attack as she witnessed our prank!

Ed delivered all of this absolutely deadpan but, crucially, without ever looking angry or raising his voice. He then said, "I think it was pretty funny actually, and he probably deserved it, but I have been instructed to belt you so get your hands up." That "I have been instructed to" bit is crucial to what happened next.

I was first up, and as he raised the belt over his shoulder, I could see the start of a grin forming on his lips as he slowly let the belt drop onto my grateful palms. After administering two of these show punishments to each of us, he told us to get back to our classes and to stay away from the pond in future. Legend!

One of the reasons for having to move on quickly from the aftermath of the decision-making process was the early appearance of "the end is nigh" warnings from the teachers. Once study leave had finished, we had another few days of generally dossing around before the official start of fifth year, which comprised of the last two weeks of term. Despite repeated warnings that these two weeks were vitally important, and that the real work started here, our young minds were already fixated on August, as everybody knows that's when the real school year starts. Anyway, they could say what they liked about those two weeks because for me, there was only one of them left!

Back in the days before extreme political correctness and the inexorable rise of the nanny state, your parents could take you out of school any time they wanted for family holidays. This wasn't overly important if your parents worked in jobs that routinely took the traditional trades holidays, as they all fell within our summer-holiday period anyway, but then, as now, for people with flexible holidays it was an eminently sensible financial decision to take them outwith peak times, i.e. outwith the school holidays. And so, that year, our entire family – me, Mum, Dad, Tommy, Pat and Gail – headed off to a rented house in Lossiemouth for a week.

The only sign that I was taking my new upper-school responsibilities seriously was that I took our newly set English novel, *Prester John*, with me and I resolved to read a chapter a night. Some chance! Well, actually, no chance as it turned out, but worse was to befall those plans as the real start of fifth year beckoned...

CHAPTER 7

Just enough education to perform

(1975–1977)

A chapter a night? Every night? What was I thinking? Anyway, when the new school year really kicked off in August not only did I not read a chapter a night, I couldn't even read the book as it had mysteriously disappeared over the summer! Now, clearly, I couldn't confess this to Cath so I just kept claiming to have forgotten it in class and somehow managed to complete any assignments relating to the novel by reading some chapter summaries that Cath handed out. Yes, I'd kept up with the Joneses, though it hadn't actually occurred to me until writing this that, except for Ma Mudie's brief and ever-so-posh tenure in first year, Cath was responsible for my English language and literature development all the way through. So, if this book is any good, thanks, Cath. Alternatively, if it's illiterate nonsense, what were you thinking, Mrs Jones?

Actually, that phrase (what were you thinking, Mrs Jones?) is also appropriate for the priceless entertainment offered up by Cath that I alluded to in an earlier chapter…

Remember when English teachers used to make you read out loud? Exactly *why* is open to speculation. To check you *could* read? To make sure you actually *did* read? To cause maximum embarrassment to adolescent boys? To keep us quiet? My personal theory is all of the above, plus it meant that the teacher didn't have to do anything much while you were reading out loud! Fair play to Cath though, she did take her turn and that is what proved her downfall.

I'm not sure how well I can describe this in writing, as it's most definitely an aural blooper, but let's give it a go… While reading a passage from whichever obscure, boring, yet in all probability academically worthy book she was currently inflicting upon us, she pronounced spoon-fed as… spoonfd. Does that work in print? Try saying it out loud… It was the kind of error that simply crashed through your senses and irrespective of how hard you were trying not to listen, and we usually tried pretty hard, you heard it loud and clear. Or I did at least.

I looked at her instantly – she never missed a beat, not a flicker of emotion, recognition or, crucially, correction as she ploughed on regardless. I looked at one or two of my friends – they'd heard it too and we exchanged knowing smirks that magnified into heavily stifled giggles. Since we were all absolutely petrified of her, we somehow managed to collectively internalise this hilarity until we left the room, but it wasn't easy. And, of course, nobody felt brave enough to point out her error. Maybe it was just an innovative teaching technique, maybe to see if we were really listening or to somehow challenge our critical abilities in a way that couldn't happen if we were simply spoonfd? Aye, right! Again, what were you thinking, Mrs Jones?

Still, there was more to fifth year than nonsense novels, missing or otherwise. Incidentally, it finally turned up bizarrely under my bed, around a month after we were supposed to hand it back!

Unfortunately, my unbroken run of mathematical success under my mentor Ed had been brought to an end and my Mathematics career came under the direction of Mrs Marshall. Long blonde hair, tight jumpers, short skirts, what wasn't to like? But another one not to be messed with.

Thankfully I still had the lovely Eleanor Masson for Chemistry, but Mushki had yielded to Barry "Boris" Crawshaw for Physics – now Boris was great but, as Head of Physics, he ran his department like a military operation and treated his pupils in much the same way. Everything was curt and efficient, and he insisted on calling everyone by their surname, including his colleagues. Much to our amusement, of course.

Biology went old-school too as we 5O – as in five O, schoolie shorthand for fifth-year O grade – students came under the wing of Dr Cook, or Sammy as he was affectionately known, despite his actual name being Jim! Sammy was close to retirement but another one not to be messed with.

I still remember the silence that fell upon us one day when he asked what the function of bone marrow was. Philip Davidson, Pip, raised his hand excitedly and, when summoned to answer, said, "Dogs eat it." We thought he was dead, but Sammy, to his credit, realising the response was genuine even though completely absurd, didn't bat an eyelid as he dismissed that gently and asked for any other ideas. That was a narrow escape for Pip, though the whole episode kept us amused for weeks.

If the previous year had contained rites of passage, this was the time when my metaphorical butterfly really started to metamorphose. During the course of fifth year I finally plucked up the courage to ask out the girl I'd first taken a shine to in the first few weeks of first year. Well, no sense in rushing these things! Needless to say there was much agonising and many sleepless nights thinking about how best to go about this, but once I'd finally decided that the deed had to be done, I decided that the best course of action was to phone her. From a phone box of course (remember them?) as there was no way I was going to risk the embarrassment of being overheard by my parents on the home phone.

I don't know what finally triggered this monumental act of bravery, but it probably involved my mates telling me to "put up or shut up" and just get on with it. Anyway, what was the worst that could happen? Well… she could say no… and tell all her mates… and ritually humiliate me in the process, so, no pressure then.

After spending a good few evenings walking back and forward past the phone box, even going in a few times, probably even dialling then quickly hanging up a few times too, the big moment finally arrived. After rehearsing my meticulously prepared ad-libs yet again, and taking a final few deep breaths, I slowly dialled her number, the phone rang a few times, then… her mum answered – darn! I calmly asked to speak to Sheena and, when she came on, she didn't even seem surprised that I was phoning her. So I was that transparent then, though it was inevitable after four and a half years I guess.

Continuing to be surprisingly calm, focused and humorous, I asked her if she'd like to go out sometime and she unhesitatingly said yes. So far, so good, but in my detailed and meticulous preparations, I hadn't actually figured out how to deal with a positive response. To be fair, I didn't have a plan to deal with a negative response either but right now that was totally irrelevant as she'd said yes – YES! Right, pull yourself together, Gordon, and don't blow this with another bout of crippling indecision.

"What about the pictures?" was the best I could come up with.

"Yeah, OK," she replied.

Without dragging this romantic tale out for too long, it was clear that we'd both exhausted our supplies of cool at this stage and, realising that neither of us knew what was actually on at the pictures, we simply agreed that we'd decide later. And that was that, the deed was done, finally. How easy was that? Why had I put it off for so long?

Unfortunately, I've completely forgotten what happened the next day at school, though I think we probably just shyly smiled at each other outside the lockers, but somehow we managed to finalise a day and a film and arranged which bus we'd meet on. Again, my memory fails over the film we chose but that's probably because we didn't actually get in! Whatever we went to see was sold out so, despite Dundee having several other cinemas, we just got on the next bus back and went to her house for a coffee. Which was way more than I'd bargained for at the outset of the evening, as this involved meeting her mum, being scrutinised with suspicion by her sister, teased by her wee brother, ignored by her dad and growled at by her dog. Still, it was a start.

There was a hiccup on the football front during this year when we found ourselves without a school team to play in as no teacher wanted to organise it. Not for the first time, I wasn't having that and went straight to the top, the Heidie, "Big Jim" Lacey, to complain.

"Right," he said, "I'll take the team. Get your pals together for training after school tomorrow."

Result!

I rounded the boys up and Big Jim rolled out in his old rugby trackie and proceeded to shout us around various running drills then supervise a game where he played in goal. Well, he was a rugby player in his day so it was the best place for him. Things were looking up then, but quickly came crashing to a halt a few days later when he declared that he didn't really have the time to take our team after all. His counter proposal was, "You do it," and I eagerly accepted the second player-manager position of my fledgling career (remember P4?).

He said he'd square it with Willie Simmons who, when confronted with an order from his boss, didn't really have much choice but to agree. So I set about collecting together my band of misfits and cobbled together a team, which didn't win many games but we had a lot of fun in the process. Not that I was thinking there was much fun involved in this football lark during the game where I broke my nose while challenging for a header – oh the sairness! I don't remember any supervising teacher being too concerned though somebody may have suggested getting it checked out.

Immediately on returning home my mum wheeched me along to the doctor's house – aye, that was when doctors were doctors – and he delivered his carefully considered medical opinion – "I think it's broken." He then said we should go to the hospital to get it checked out the next day, which we duly did.

After the requisite wait in A&E, a doctor arrived and enquired, "What seems to be the matter with you?"

To which I replied, "I think my nose is broken."

He adjusted his seating position, slowly leaned forward and firmly grabbed my nose – again, oh the sairness!

As I yelped in agony he leaned back and simply said, "Yes, it's broken."

Through my haze of pain, worse than when it actually happened, I thought, *Well, if it wisnae broken before, then it certainly is now!*

He continued, "We'll have another look in six weeks' time, but if it's a clean break, we won't have to do anything other than wait for it to heal."

When I enquired as to what would happen if it didn't heal naturally, he nonchalantly replied, "Then we'll break it again and set it straight."

What? This didn't sound great to me, so I was really hoping that it would just set itself naturally. My instructions were to avoid all physical contact for six weeks, and no sport – so no football, basketball or volleyball. Thankfully all went well and, six weeks later, having received the all-clear for normal activities to resume, my first test was to be basketball practice after school. I wasn't in the slightest worried about this as, although basketball has quite a lot of physical contact, I'd never experienced anything untoward.

As I opened the games-hall door, somebody behind me spoke and, as I turned to answer him, one of my teammates yelled from inside, "Welcome back," so I turned again, just in time to receive a basketball at full pelt straight in my coupon! Again, oh the sairness! This time, thankfully, the pain subsided really quickly and, having ascertained that no fresh damage had been done, normal activities were indeed resumed.

The highlight of the year, without question, was when a charity game was arranged between a school XI and Dundee United, to be played at Carnoustie Panmure's ground, Westfield Park. This was huge on so many levels. One, it was Dundee United. Dundee United! OK, it was their S (schoolboy) signings, but it was still Dundee United. Two, it was to be played at Westfield. This was a proper park, with barriers and goal nets and paying spectators and everything. Three, it was Dundee United!

After the fixture was announced there was a nerve-wracking period before the team was selected, and the fact that it was to be a school XI increased the tension as it meant there had to be representatives from every year of the school, thus cutting down the number of places available to each year. I shouldn't have really been worried as I'm sure they couldn't not have selected the senior team's player-manager, but until the team was announced there were no guarantees and, well, we're all very well aware of my capacity for fretting about decisions by now.

From a purely football point of view, selecting a team in such a way poses many problems. If you're simply picking the best player or two from each year, what happens if they're all strikers or, worse, goalkeepers? Thankfully it wasn't as extreme as that in the end but there were still some pragmatic decisions to be made. One of which involved me playing completely out of position in the most important game of my career to date.

In a way it made sense, since they were clearly going to be better than us and one way to minimise the potential damage was to play your strongest players in defence. And so, setting aside my creative and goalscoring urges, I became, for one night only, a centre back. I played well too, and took great pleasure in noting that my man, their centre forward, didn't score. The fact that his buddies managed to rattle in nine goals didn't deflect from my achievement, nonetheless.

Apart from the scoreline, obviously, I loved everything about that game, but I was so tired afterwards. Partly because it was a big pitch, partly because we were doing so much running to match these budding professionals, partly because us senior players were doing even more running to cover our younger colleagues, and partly due to the sheer emotional drain of playing in what was, for us in general and me in particular, such a huge game.

My principal mind's eye memory of the game involves cutting out a long through ball in the second half by controlling it on my chest, taking a touch then dummying one of their forwards to buy the time to curl a beautifully executed pass down the line to our right winger. Poetry in motion. And right in front of the dugouts too, right in front of the legendary United manager, Jim McLean.

Someone who'd been standing within earshot told me later that Jim had commented during the game that "that boy can play", and he was referring to me! Ah, Jim, if only you'd followed that interest up. He did have another chance, mind, and he wasn't the only professional coach to make that observation, but modesty prevents me from going into detail on that. Well, not just now anyway...

But this was the year that my hitherto unhindered academic prowess was called into question for the first time. The Highers were, indeed, turning out to be a bit more intensive and demanding than anything that had gone before and most people appeared to have stepped up their efforts accordingly. The trouble was, I'd never previously put in any conscious effort so didn't recognise the need.

I stumbled through the prelims with reasonable but not fantastic marks, proving that innate ability still counted for something, but this was the first sign of an intellectual wobble. Well, not really an intellectual one as that was still not in question, but the warning signs regarding work rate were most definitely being posted.

The fragrant Mrs Masson was the main one to attempt to bring it to my attention. Having scored something in the high 50s (%) for Chemistry, on returning the paper she enquired, "Well, what do you think?"

"Not bad for a prelim", was my somewhat ill-advised, uncharacteristically smug-sounding and less than well-considered reply. She went spare, absolutely berserk at me – rather unkindly, I thought at the time.

On the spot I manufactured some theory that by not putting in any special work for my prelims the results would give me a better indication of what I actually knew, allowing me to then concentrate on my weaknesses between then and the Highers. Unfortunately the main weakness in this theory lay in me actually believing this tripe. She wasn't impressed, not at all, and told me so in no uncertain manner. Having sulked for probably about all of 30 seconds, normal service was quickly resumed and I returned to my carefree approach to life in general, focussing my attention on my principal obsessions of football, music and Sheena...

Our "romance" was trotting gently along without really progressing in any noticeable or meaningful way. We'd probably see each other once a week, twice was a novelty, never more. We didn't even really hang out that much at school, as that would've been too embarrassing, but we appeared to be happy. I used to get teased mercilessly by two of her friends, Susan and Debbie, who were in sixth year but in my Higher Chemistry class. They all played hockey together, all good players, and I guess they gave her as hard a time as they did me, but I have no way of knowing for certain. Girls do tend to band together and, even now, it's hard to penetrate their inner circle. Ooo, err, missus!

Our biggest adventure was to go on holiday together, and that certainly sent Susan and Debbie's imaginations into overdrive. It was, however, all perfectly innocent. Whether I thought it up or whether it was my parents' idea is long gone from memory, but it was decided that I could invite Sheena to come with us for a long weekend in Campbeltown...

Dad's friend Alec, he of the Victoria Hotel in Nairn, had by this time also acquired the Argyll Arms Hotel in Campbeltown and we had started alternating between the two hotels for holidays. One of our early family visits was memorable as it was the first, and so far only, time that I've steered a boat! I've no idea why Alec even had a boat, but he did, and he invited me and Dad to go out with him one day for a wee cruise around Campbeltown Loch which, I can reliably report, is not "full of whisky"!

After exiting the harbour under his expert (?) control, he duly handed the reins – I know that's not the nautically correct term! – to my even less-expert hands with my only instruction being, "Just keep heading for that island over there."

Aye, aye captain!

Anyway, while Alec took my dad below deck – I'm getting the hang of this sailor-speak here! – to show him the inner workings and accommodation, I suppose, I accepted my navigation responsibility and just kept the boat on course for what I now know, courtesy of Google Maps, to be Davaar Island.

As the island came ever nearer, I started to get a wee bit concerned that the two responsible adults onboard had not returned to check what I was doing – I was fully aware that I didn't really know what I was doing – and eventually shouted to tell Alec that we were getting gey close to the island. He hurtled through the door muttering something like "Jesus Christ!", grabbed the wheel and turned us away from the island towards the open sea. "I forgot to tell you to turn," was the only explanation offered, but as no harm had been done, no great fuss was made and we completed our wee jaunt safely under his command.

On another never-to-be-forgotten occasion we even split the time between the two hotels, necessitating the horrendous journey from Campbeltown to Nairn which, although it's only a bit over 200 miles, probably took about six hours on the windy roads of the Kintyre Peninsula then up the Great Glen and suchlike.

Anyway, Sheena agreed so, to keep everything above board, my dad spoke to her mum, assured her of her daughter's complete safety, received her blessing and the grand trip was on. We were well supervised and the main thing that sticks in my memory of the trip was that Scotland v England was on the TV on the Saturday afternoon! Who said romance was dead?

Sheena went out shopping with my mum, no stereotyping here then, while me, Dad and Alec watched the game.

For the record, though I don't specifically remember this, it must've been the 1976 game at Hampden, which we won 2–1 and was decided by that epic Kenny Dalglish trickler through Ray Clemence's legs. On researching this fact I realise that this whole trip must've taken place after our Highers were finished, as I don't think either set of parents would've sanctioned anything interfering with our studying. Well, I say "studying" though I've already documented that that was proving to be a problem for me...

With the not-too-ringing endorsement of my prelim efforts still in my mind, I did try to do some revision for my Highers. I had, I think, by this time accepted that putting in some extra effort was the only sensible way ahead. We'd long grown out of that whole swot mentality, other than pretty much purely in jest, and people were definitely staying in and, well, studying. So I did too. At least I stayed in, most of the time.

The trouble was I genuinely didn't know what to do. I'd never done it before and this was now a culture shock. So I'm pretty sure most of my studying consisted of me reading over some notes and either deciding that I already knew that or panicking because I didn't and wasn't going to change anything now!

Well, the result of all of this was that the straight A student turned overnight into a straight B student. Except that's not really a recognisable phrase, is it? It wasn't even factually accurate as I stumbled to a C grade in Physics. In my own mind I do actually still count this as a B however, as the main reason for that C was the most monumental piece of stupidity I ever committed in any academic setting. That distinction – the academic setting – is only to allow for other acts of equally, or indeed greater, monumental stupidity in other contexts yet to come.

Anyway, at that time, all of the science papers followed the same pattern – Paper 1 was multiple-choice; Paper 2 was written, extended responses. I reached the end of the Physics Paper 2 probably about 30–40 minutes before the end of the allotted time. Deciding that a couple of the questions may benefit from further analysis and possible addition, I divided this remaining time between considering those options and idly looking around watching other people. At the end, I thought I'd done alright, not great, but probably a B and maybe even an A.

When we gathered outside for the ritual post-exam inquest, one of my mates asked what I'd written for the last question – "You know, the one on electronics."

"What question on electronics?" I blurted out as I realised… I… hadn't… turned… the… last… page… over!

What a completely idiotic mistake to make. My specialist subject, in the Physics context, in which I could have guaranteed full marks and… I hadn't done it. Amateur mistake, talk about self-destruction.

Still, I did have the consolation of balancing out that underachievement with a strolling A in my O grade Biology exam, thus proving that that level definitely did mark the end point of my effortless intellect. Oh well, lessons learned, onwards and upwards.

Obviously, the end of fifth year heralded… the beginning of sixth year and yet more choices to be made – cue the same old agonising feelings of indecision returning to haunt every waking minute. Despite my apparent downward curve, I decided to stick with what had previously been my strengths. So, for sixth year, the choices ended up as CSYS Mathematics, CSYS Chemistry, Higher Biology and… O grade French. Wait, what? Well, there does come a point where you can't ignore reality anymore, and this particular reality was that if I was going to go to university, then I needed a language. So, desperately trying to eradicate the memories of Miss Doig, it was back to trying to recreate my halcyon days of four years previously, and conquer French. Once again, the old "sixth year starts now" and "it's not long until your exams" warnings came thick and fast and, once again, we all paid absolutely zero attention and focused instead on the upcoming summer holiday, the legendary summer of '76…

Maybe we were all beginning to realise that this probably didn't last forever, I'm not sure. Obviously we were aware of the dwindling of our number. It hadn't been so noticeable the year before, as most of the people who left were, how do I put this, less academically inclined and therefore mainly not in our immediate peer group anyway. That's not to appear snobbish in any way – it's just a fact.

Of my closest friends, off the top of my head I can only think of one who left at the end of fourth year. It's a natural consequence of setting classes – if you're always in the top set, you're going to mix with the other academically able kids and drift away from the others who were perhaps closer to you in primary school. Anyway, it's different at the end of fifth year as many academically able people decide to venture into the world of work, or go to university at that first available opportunity, but for the rest of us there remained the prospect of one more year swanning around as part of the school elite.

As preparation for this final year, I had my first real taste of employment that summer. Not sure how it came about, but I acquired the position of Car Park Attendant in the grassy car park opposite the railway station, the very one I had learned to ride a bike without stabilisers in all those years ago. Come on, keep up. I was on a six-days-on, six-days-off rotation with some old guy who smoked a pipe. Our only interplay was to meet up on the handover day to, well, hand over the tickets and the change pouch.

Although sitting on your backside in a wee hut all day sounds like a cushy number, it doesn't quite tell the full story. One, the wee hut was exactly that, a wee hut. It was around three-foot square with a horse-box door on the front, no windows. Two, there wasn't a chair inside, just a wooden bench. Three, there was no insulation. I know it was summer, but this is the north-east coast of Scotland. And four, the hours of business were 8.30 a.m. to 5.30 p.m. No breaks, no toilet facilities, go figure!

Apart from the excruciating boredom, it was fantastic! Even now, summer of '76 chart music could be my specialist *Mastermind* subject as my only companion during each unremitting nine-hour stint was Wonderful Radio One. Some of my friends used to drop by, and my mum would occasionally turn up, especially if I'd forgotten to bring my lunch or whatever, but most of the time it was just me and my radio.

The only time I alternated from Radio One was on the Saturday of the Wimbledon Final, when I willed my tennis hero Ilie Năstase to beat Björn Borg. Now Borg was pretty cool, but he wasn't Năstase, the George Best of tennis. Anyway, Borg won (and continued to do so for five straight years) and Năstase never reached the final again despite being clearly and obviously the most talented player of his generation. Well, that's my opinion anyway. I admired Borg's efficiency, and he became my favourite as Năstase faded, but once he retired, I kind of lost interest in tennis as they all became a bit samey. Edberg was pretty good but only Federer has enticed me to watch much tennis since.

Hey, that was the first digression for a while; I must be getting the hang of this writing lark, but let's get back to 1976.

My other regular visitors that summer were my two newly acquired groupies, Diana and Hilary. OK, maybe groupies is a wee over-exaggeration! I have absolutely no recollection of how it started but the two of them used to drop by for a chat most days. I even hung out with them a couple of times at night, including one time when the three of us went back to Diana's house when her parents were away on holiday – calm yer scanties, it was all perfectly innocent!

I remember it well – we just sat around talking and drinking coffee, and it was probably the most relaxed I'd ever felt in female company, probably because I had absolutely no inclination that there were any romantic thoughts being nurtured.

Later, when the two of them went away on holiday somewhere up north together for a week, probably with one set of parents, they even sent me a postcard. Now, call me thick, but… it genuinely never occurred to me that this was part of a mating ritual and that Diana actually had a fancy for me, and that Hilary was her more confident wingman. In hindsight this is now perfectly clear but, since the whole thing went clean over my head, she eventually lost interest and moved on. Strange thing was, I liked her! Even stranger thing was that my dad told me that Diana liked me – how on earth did he know? I just told him he was havering and didn't give it a second thought. Oh well, missed opportunities and all that.

Although the job had some attractions, great earning potential was not among them. The only fringe benefit was to resell some discarded tickets. Every day, I would patrol my estate looking for tickets that drivers had carelessly discarded and, provided they looked OK, i.e. not covered in mud (or worse), soaked or completely frayed, then I would take those back to the hut. Those that made the cut then became mine, and therefore, the proceeds of their resale became mine too. It definitely didn't make my fortune but it did provide a wee bonus, not to mention the distraction of finding the tickets in the first place.

My fiddle was nothing compared to one of the guys working the other car park near the golf course. He raised enough to buy a racing bike purely out of his ill-gotten gains! He did have a much busier car park, but I would never have had the bottle to squeeze that amount out of the deal!

Anyway, for our evening entertainment, we would therefore constantly look for cost-cutting opportunities. And so it was that Andrew Menzies – Mince – and myself used to head off to the Monifieth discos on a Friday evening, on foot. Carnoustie to Monifieth is around four miles, and most of the time we walked home too. In the dark. I think we sometimes got the bus home, but we didn't pay to get in so, all in all, it was a cheap night out.

Our free entry was courtesy of a mate who was helping to run the café, which was basically just a wee room with juice and crisps to sell from a box. Fortunately for us, it had an easily accessible outside window which he would usher us through when nobody official was looking.

By this time we were easily among the older groovers in the place as most of our peers, and us to be fair, had given up going one or two years previously. We were now revisiting our relative youth simply for something to do, and because it was free. Also, being slightly older, it did give us a certain cachet with some of the girls, at least the ones who weren't thinking, *What the hell are they doing here?* Not that I recall us having any meaningful success at this time, but it did while away a Friday evening.

During this summer I also had my first experience of overindulging in alcohol. It was accidental, and it wasn't too severe, but it was definitely an experience.

One night, a few of us ventured into the Brax Hotel in Carnoustie. Clearly we were all underage, but probably in common with most small towns, the recognised underagers' bar seemed to rotate around the town, and at this particular point, the Brax held the baton. I didn't drink, staunchly and famously at the time. Not only were my parents devout non-drinkers, but I still believed I was going to play professional football, and professional athletes don't drink. Or they shouldn't. But this night I had a couple of lagers and also my one and only sip to date of Guinness. Yuch! Like muddy pondwater. Not that I've sampled muddy pondwater you understand, but it tasted how I'd imagine that to.

Anyway, we had a great night and I strolled happily back up the road without really realising that I was... a wee bit merry shall we say? Nothing extreme, but I now had to face Mum and Dad. No problem, carefully say the goodnights and head off to bed... Well, that was the plan, but this was the night that I had to cash up and prepare my car-park takings for banking in the morning. And Mum always helped me... not because I needed her help, just because she enjoyed counting change – everybody's got to have a hobby, I suppose! I think she just liked handling coins. You should've seen her in action on the puggy machines, but only with coppers, mind, never silver.

Anyway, counting that lot out without giving the game away was a challenge but, to the best of my knowledge, I somehow got away with it and lived to tell the tale unscathed. (Applying some long-distance, mature hindsight, it couldn't possibly have gone unnoticed but, for whatever reason, nothing was ever said.)

Soon, another summer had been and gone and went, and it was time to return to school. This time though, we were the crème de la crème, the elite – we were sixth years. It was exciting. Suddenly we had privileges. We had more time off, we were only required to be in when we had classes, we had the run of our own common room, and there were only about 20-odd of us, an almost equal male–female split.

One of our first events was an upper-school assembly during which the Rector, Jim Lacey, would announce the prefects for the year. We sat there sniggering away as he called out the obvious candidates to receive their badge and red tie on the stage. This was deemed to be a great honour and he was milking it for all it was worth. Then, still playing in my mind somewhere, I heard him call my name. I suppose I never realised my place in the scheme of things at that time. Why would I not be a prefect? Primary school dux, straight A student (OK, minor blip in fifth year downgrading that temporarily to straight B), principled campaigner and player-manager of the senior football team – obvious choice really, with that increasingly overworked hindsight. But I really did not expect this.

Gathering my thoughts quickly I made my way up sheepishly to receive my awards, and as he handed over the tie Big Jim said, "It's better than the one you're wearing."

Before I could stop myself I whispered back, "You think so?" – this could've been construed as insolence, though it really wasn't, but Jim was a good man and simply smiled indulgently as I strolled off. So, I really was part of the elite now.

My one last revolutionary act was to ignore his advice about the tie and I continued to wear my beautiful blue silk number that I was exceptionally proud of. My continuing sartorial bolshieness was, however, brought to a swift halt the next week when I happened to encounter Jim in the corridor.

"Morning, sir," said I.

"Morning, Gordon," he replied, "and you *will* have your prefect's tie on tomorrow…" without breaking stride. His menacing demeanour told me that there was to be no more debate or evasion on this subject without serious consequences for my health. And so the blue tie was consigned to the back of the wardrobe.

They say power corrupts and, I have to admit, elements of our prefectship certainly went to our heads. One of our duties was, on a rota basis, to go down to the junior and middle school areas at interval and lunchtime and help the Heads of School to supervise. In practice, the teachers went to their office for a coffee and we acted out our Clint Eastwood vigilante fantasies!

This led to some fantastic conflicts, especially with the fourth-year neds. If they were congregating in their cloak-room or toilet areas, we were supposed to "move them along" by "encouraging" them not to loiter and to go outside. Nowhere in the script were we permitted to use physical violence, or the threat thereof but, as I said, power corrupts.

One classic instance stands out in my mind, when one of the more obnoxious ones decided not to move from his slouched position on a radiator despite repeated requests. Memory clouds the exact detail of what followed, in that it may have been me or it may have been my friend Barry – Baz – but one of us neatly swept his feet away, causing him to go horizontal about three feet from the ground then crash to earth in a painfully uncontrolled manner. Not best pleased.

I actually think it was me, and it's not something I'm proud of, but the reason I'm hesitating over claiming culpability is that this particular ned later exacted revenge on Baz in a spectacular fashion.

As the winter of their discontent peaked during the snow season, a group of us headed off to engage them in a snow-ball fight. Not the most considered plan for law enforcers, granted, but it seemed like a good idea at the time. In the ensuing battle, Baz clocked one at point-blank range straight into his coupon. Bad enough if it was an ordinary snowball, as compressed solid ice isn't a particularly forgiving material, but when spiked with rocks it's an altogether more potent weapon. Almost a weapon of Baz destruction as it turned out, hand-delivered by radiator boy!

Sixth year was great, but it was the start of me beginning to question things. I suppose it was the realisation that a chapter was ending and the uncertainty and unfamiliarity of the future was rapidly approaching.

Early on in the year we were forced to confront the future when we were pressed into the UCCA form procedure. Nowadays UCCA (Universities Central Council on Admissions) has transformed into UCAS (Universities and Colleges Admissions Service), but the principle remains the same, I think. Basically this is a centralised mechanism for candidates indicating their university preferences and being matched with the university's requirements. This required some clarity of thought about my future career, a clarity that was obvious only by its absence. It had always been taken for granted that I was going to university, and equally assumed it would be the local university, but no thought at all had ever gone into the crucial "to do what" part. You can guess what's coming – yes, here we go with the extended agonising and sleepless nights again.

This time, the "don't want to disappoint" element had an extra dimension because there appeared to be an unspoken assumption that I would somehow follow in my dad's and brother's footsteps by becoming an upmarket sparkie, an electronics engineer. The only problem with this was that, in the absence of knowing what I did want to do, and unusually for me, I was becoming increasingly clear in my own mind about what I didn't want to do. And that was to be an electronics engineer. Not that I had any clue what that job entailed, but I really hadn't sparked (bad pun, not intended but left in for comic effect) with electronics when it came up in the Physics syllabus.

Influenced by my colourful introduction to Mathematics by Uncle Ed, and beguiled by the effortlessly cool demeanour of my CSYS Mathematics teacher "Bungalow" Bill Sinclair, I was increasingly attracted to Mathematics as the only pure science. Not irretrievably attracted, mind, this is me remember, but certainly veering towards. Yet, I also had some kind of hankering for Chemistry and Biology – what to do?

In the end the predominant advice was that, because biological sciences were in higher demand than the physical sciences, including Mathematics, should I be accepted to a biological science course then I could always change my mind and take up the less popular physical science option without a problem. Result!

This revelation meant that I could put off the decision for another few months in the vague hope that inspiration would finally strike and all would eventually become clear.

This was to be a pattern, or a modus operandi, that I would revisit several times in the future. Hence, influenced by my two disappointed prospective GP friends, I opted to apply to study Pharmacology at the University of Dundee. Eh? Pharmacology? Where did that come from? What was I thinking? I barely knew what it was!

I did, however, have more of an idea than my dear departed grandmother who, on relating proudly to one of my aunts that, "Oor Gordon's going to university. He's doing Pharmacology. I don't know where he's got that from though – we've never had any farmers in the family!"

Priceless. Not to worry, Gran. Pharmacology was never going to be a goer, but we'll return to that later.

I've skipped a little ahead of myself here. My teacher allocation for this final year was pretty good. The aforementioned Bungalow Bill Sinclair took our main CSYS Mathematics class, and he was completely different to any other teacher we'd encountered. He really lived for Mathematics and had a particularly cutting line in wit that we thought sarcastic while he preferred ironic. Whatever, he did influence us all in taking our sarcasm/irony up a level or two, and on a serious note, he influenced me in making me realise that maybe, just maybe, Mathematics was my thing. I loved it, and I was totally taken in by his "the only pure science" assertion. Mainly as I could see it was true – everything depends on Mathematics. I would later describe it myself as "truth, beauty and logic", and I still believe that.

He neatly encapsulated the thrill that you can get from solving or proving something mathematically, describing it as "aesthetically pleasing". Wow!

I was also doing another minor CSYS Mathematics paper, Statistics, but that class consisted entirely of me and Sheena. Distracted or what? Especially when we were in one of our off phases, which I'll expand on soon enough.

Stewart Ramsay was our teacher and, unfairly as I thought at the time, he would cancel the class if I was absent but not if Sheena was off. He said it was unprofessional for him to be in a classroom alone with only a sixth-year girl. Probably quite wise really.

For Chemistry we came under the wings of Andy Masson (no relation to the lovely Eleanor), Kenny Ward (the extrovert Head of Department) and Derek Weston. Andy was hard to understand as he barely moved his mouth when he spoke. I used to think it was because his beard was too tight. Ken was a real character, a lovely man who added another layer of humour to our already expanding repertoire. Derek was a very serious man. We used to call him the Doc, or sometimes, for reasons long gone, Batman.

Biology proved to be an interesting experience, with Dr "Sunshine" Dalrymple. Now he was indeed a "chap". He dressed very dapperly in a three-piece suit and carried a cane with, I'm sure I remember, a wolf's head on the handle. Not a real head, obviously. That would be bizarre. No, it was just a silver carving. Anyway, the point was that his mannerisms, and use of that cane, were very strange and that in itself was enough to keep us in check.

He used to sit on the edge of his demonstration desk at the front of the class, tapping his cane on the ground as he surveyed us or using it to point at one of us when he required our input. There was a centre aisle perpendicular to his desk, and from his vantage point, my location was back left while one of my friends, Bobby, was front right, and therefore very close to Sunshine.

One warm day, he was droning on about something and, while I was watching and listening to him, I could see Bobby starting to sway on his stool. Gently, almost imperceptibly at first, but gathering momentum. I also noticed that his eyes appeared to be shut. I think we probably began to nudge each other, stifling our giggles, before Bobby suddenly, yet in slow motion, began to keel over, dropping like a stone onto the floor. Cue stunned silence, eventually broken by Sunshine leaning forward slightly and gently saying, "Bobby? Bobby? Are you alright, Bobby?"

Of course he's not alright, you clown – he's just toppled off a three-foot high stool onto a solid floor! Thankfully Bobby came round quickly enough with no lasting damage, other than our constant references to the spectacle he'd caused!

There were maybe half a dozen of us in that Higher class from sixth year, and we probably spent most of the time trying to impress the fifth-year girls – I certainly impressed Patti… a fact that would only explicitly come to light that New Year when we locked lips in a Monifieth street at around three in the morning!

Patti was gorgeous, all dark hair and smouldering eyes in a very '70s rock chick kind of way, but natural. She used to laugh about how fast I spoke – really? – and did tell me one time that I had lovely arms. It's always nice to be appreciated, and I can recognise now that she was flirting with me, and I really liked her, but I was "with girlfriend" at this stage, I think? Yes, the romance with Sheena that had taken a long time to start had developed into a bit of an on–off–on saga, and I can only surmise that it must've been on at the point where I was ignoring signs of interest from Patti…

That only leaves French, and it was a bit of a flashback to second year to be reacquainted with the now Head of Department, Alan Wolfe. I was the only sixth-year candidate in a class of around half a dozen not-so-bright fifth-year repeats, all boys. That's more than a little unkind, as their record was probably no worse than mine, but I would bet that none of them had been coasting along at 95% or thereabouts until taken down by Miss Doig. Grr!

With hindsight, yet again, that attitude didn't help me too much as I coasted along in that company, clearly superior to the rest of them, and reverted to type in that I did just enough to get by. Almost less than enough actually, because I used to miss the odd class as it seemed all too easy this time around. Anyway, hoisted by this particular petard I only scraped by with the minimum of achievement at the end which I could justify to myself by saying, "Job done, university admission requirements satisfied."

It was still a monumental underachievement, and one that I regret to this day. *C'est la vie*! Thinking back though, I wonder just exactly how bored the exam markers got of reading the identical opening sentence in every, literally, O grade French essay – "*Par un beau jour d'été pendant les grandes vacances...*"

But at least that was a pass. The downward trajectory that had kicked in over the last few years continued unchecked as the straight A student reached the dizzy depths of straight D! I say straight D but that can only be justified by virtue of balancing my Higher Biology B and O grade French C against my CSYS Statistics E – *E*? That only left the Mathematics and Chemistry to maintain the D average and you have one pretty grim set of results for a prodigal genius. Worst of all, the lesson still hadn't truly sunk in yet...

On the upside, our social lives started to develop somewhat during sixth year and some of our more adventurous peers started to host unsupervised parties. It's funny because, at the time of writing this, I've just watched a TV programme where Kevin Bridges, a young stand-up comedian, does a sketch about the difference between traditional American spring break parties and the "empties" he was used to in Coatbridge. Whether Kevin has any longevity as a comedian, and is therefore still recognised when you're reading this, is anybody's guess, though I suspect he will, because he's funny. [*2020 update: He has, he is, it's not, I was right and... he is, very!*] Whether this story has any longevity, and will be read at all, is probably even more in doubt.

Basically, he weaves his story around the contrasts between the sanitised, organised, alcohol-light or alcohol-free, happy, upbeat events favoured by young Americans, and the chaotic, threatening and often downright dangerous, alcohol-fuelled parties he knows as "empties", so-called because the relevant parents are away and the house is therefore empty.

It has to be said that this comparative exercise does not show Scotland in a good light, though it is remarkably accurate. However, and it's been a while since a wee digression kicked in, our parties definitely fell somewhere between these two extremes. This may have had something to do with the inherent differences between Coatbridge and the altogether cosier and more middle-class surroundings of Carnoustie/Monifieth, but our parties were relatively tame affairs. Nothing ever got wrecked or destroyed, certainly not deliberately, and definitely nothing ever got stolen. The worst things left over for the teenage host to rectify probably involved the cleaning up of the inevitable technicolour yawns that are an obvious by-product of the teenager/alcohol mix, but even these were generally well controlled. As I remember anyway, but I never hosted a party, so what do I know?

One that sticks in my mind was at Brigitte's house one Friday evening. Not so much for the party itself, but for the next day.

Having got home around 3 a.m. or thereby, we all had to meet a bus at the school around 7.30 a.m. in order to make a 9.30 a.m. kick-off time at Blairgowrie. This was quite a big deal, as Blairgowrie wasn't one of our usual fixtures. Although only about 30 miles away, this was the equivalent of playing in Europe for us! The only other time we'd had to travel outwith the 20-mile radius that contained all of the schools in Angus and Dundee had been to visit Kirkcaldy, and that really was the other side of the moon.

Trying to catch up on our missing sleep on the bus, we kept getting annoyed by this little second-year kid leaning over the top of our seat and laughing at us. When we eventually told him to "go away", or words to that effect, he just said, "Were you at a party last night?"

"Yes, now go away," we replied, followed by, "And how do you know?"

"Because my sister looks as bad as you two this morning too!"

Out of the mouths of babes... not that he was a babe you understand; nor was his sister... oh, you know what the phrase means!

Anyway, we made it and even won the game thanks to a penalty won and converted by yours truly. It wasn't without controversy however as the penalty award was hotly disputed, with more than one of their players rather ungenerously accusing me of diving. The one who was most upset and intent on revenge was apparently still muttering dire threats when Baz said to him, "Go easy on him, mate – we were all at a party until 3 a.m.," which prompted a shrug and a "fair enough" response and the abandonment of all intent on revenge. Thanks, Baz.

There also developed what could've been construed as less than healthy relationships with a few of the teachers though, in reality, there was absolutely nothing untoward.

A core group of about six or eight of us – me, Baz, Jimmy, Big Al, Al, Jim, Smiffy – were into pretty much everything. In fact, the central core of that outer core – me, Baz, Jimmy, Al – were the mainstay of the football, volleyball and basketball teams, generally then, in hindsight, the main men, though I genuinely never, ever felt that at the time. Weird.

Anyway, the outer core, which now looks like the main men + the hangers on (sorry guys) formed pretty much the common denominator in all other activities too. Like meeting one of our favourite teachers for a few pints in various local establishments. We were on the cusp of legality, some had probably turned 18, but I'm sure the authorities would not have taken this much into consideration, even if common sense was a little more in evidence back then.

I remember the teacher marvelled at my capacity for drinking Coca-Cola (other soft drinks are available) one night as he and most of the others got slowly sozzled. Another teacher turned to our group for a bit of solace when his marriage broke up, inviting us round to his house and probably out for a few drinks too. Again, nothing untoward, but not exactly kosher if playing strictly to the rules.

More acceptable, maybe, was when we were recruited by Bungalow Bill to play the parts of Cavalry Officers in a local theatre production of *Calamity Jane*, in which he was the producer. I say recruited as there wasn't really an invitation issued, more an order. One day he just wandered into the classroom and declared that all of us were to be his Cavalry Officers and that we should report for rehearsals the next evening. How could we refuse?

I think the show ran for six nights, so we were split into two groups and played our parts on alternate nights. All we were required to do was to run on stage at the appropriate moment and scuffle with each other to try and dance with Jane, then stand in the background singing "The Black Hills of Dakota". We may have returned to the stage later to fill up some space on "Just Blew in From the Windy City" and "The Deadwood Stage", but I might be making that up.

I still think I remain the only actor (cough) to have played the part of an American Cavalry Officer while wearing red terry towelling socks. Whip-Crack-Away!

Despite this fashion faux pas, the whole experience was a riot, especially the end-of-show party which was held in a garage halfway between Arbroath and Dundee, appropriately named The Halfway Garage. More pertinently, it also happened to be almost halfway between Carnoustie and Monifieth, and as it was slightly closer to Monifieth, I arranged to stay at Baz's afterwards.

The sight of around eight of us meandering along the main Arbroath–Dundee road, not dual carriageway at that time, at six in the morning must've been something else.

After around two hours' sleep I was up and away again on the bus home to prepare for my 10.30 a.m. Sunday kick-off. I do recall that, unexpectedly and inexplicably, I played a blinder in that game!

Some of the guys in our group ended up getting a bit closer to one or two of the main luvvies than I was comfortable with, and I did wonder why these 30-ish-year-olds wanted to spend so much time with boys of 17/18, but I just gave it a miss most of the time and let them get on with it.

Good times, good times, but as I said earlier, a change was a-coming, and we knew it. We went virtually instantly from being the academic elite to the forgotten few, a nuisance that the teachers no longer wanted hanging around and no longer had time for. It's a fact of life though as, by the time we were checking out, they already had a new academic elite, a new sixth year, and we were suddenly yesterday's men. Former pupils.

Now that I was officially no longer a schoolboy, I had work to do.

CHAPTER 8

Drifting into university...

(1977–1978)

If leaving school was a big event, maybe none of us realised exactly how life-changing this period of time was actually to be. From our sheltered year at the top of the pile in sixth year, the academic elite, we were heading off into the unknown to be the new boys and girls again.

For me, my first taste of that was very early on when I turned up for my summer job. No couthie car park gig, one week on, one week off, this time round. Oh no, this was the real deal. So real, in fact, that it started at half past six in the morning. That's right, 6.30 a.m. – 0630. It doesn't matter what format you put that in, that's early. It certainly is for any teenager who has a long history of struggling to be where they're meant to be a full two and a half hours later than that!

Yes, half past six was the starting time at Carnoustie Golf Course.

To allow for breakfast and my new commute, still not too shabby at a whisker over a mile, to be completed on my trusty racing bike, my alarm was duly set for 5.30 a.m., a time of the morning that I was entirely unaware even existed. Why did I agree to this? Simply because this was the best-paying summer job in town, by a country mile. That's because it was a real, full-time job, with the staff numbers increased on a temporary basis through the peak growing and holiday season. Our working day consisted of 0630–1230 and 1330–1530, so right there was the other pay-off – early start = early finish!

Actually, successfully getting this job only happened by accident because what I had actually been aiming for was a grass-cutting job with the Carnoustie Town Council Parks Department. My friend Mince had worked with them the year before and had told me all about it, and it sounded OK, but the trouble was that you just had to apply for a summer position with the council, then see what they offered you, if anything. So the good news was, "We'd like to offer you a job," swiftly followed by the bad news, "on the golf course." Oh well…

Just what a bonus the early finish was to be became a bit obscured by the fact that I would pretty much fall asleep not that long after getting home!

Getting up in what seemed to be the middle of the night followed by a physical job and eight hours of fresh air meant one tired wee boy come knocking-off time. My normal routine at the end of the day would be to shower, have an early tea then nod off in front of Wimbledon or The Open. Suitably refreshed by the time the 6 o'clock news came on, I'd be ready to go in search of whatever the evening might bring.

As that was the summer when two or three of the boys had acquired driving licences, and the use of Daddy's car, our horizons were expanding in terms of looking for entertainment. Arbroath became a regular haunt where we used to frequent a disco run by one of the theatre chappies that one or two of my amigos had become friendly with. Like I said, I wasn't part of the inner circle of that particular arrangement but, as an integral member of the wider circle, was included in most of the activities.

One of those nights out led to a useful life lesson being learned, however. Having constantly pestered the chargehand at the golf course, Billy, for a shot at the weekend overtime, I finally made it onto his rota and was duly handed the opportunity to make some relatively easy money. The weekend gig involved turning up at 6 a.m. on both Saturday and Sunday, but only to rake the bunkers and switch the greens – a highly technical practice involving the swishing of a long cane over the greens and tees to sweep away the morning dew and any overnight worm casts and debris. Easy-peasy, two hours max, double-time pay, then back to bed. What could possibly go wrong?

Well, one outrageously late night out in Arbroath could go wrong, returning home around 3.30 a.m. slightly the worse for wear and acutely conscious of having to get up only two hours later to rake bunkers and switch greens!

Now at this point, dear reader, you're probably getting ahead of yourself and thinking *he didn't turn up*, but that would be too obvious. No, I did indeed turn up – I hauled my weary carcass down to the golf course early, if anything.

I picked up my tools and headed down the Burnside Course, raking the bunkers of the first and eighteenth holes as I went. On reaching the first tee and the eighteenth green, just outside the still-deserted Starter's Box, I was surprised but delighted to note no visible worm casts on either.

Making the wholly naïve assumption that these two specific examples could be generalised across the whole golf course, I concluded that the worms had had a night off and that I was therefore only required to rake the bunkers. Zooming round in half the allotted time meant I could be tucked up in bed again within an hour or so of leaving it, while still pocketing four hours' overtime. Fantastico!

On the Sunday morning, no such luck with the lazy worms, so I put in the full stint.

The other good thing about the weekend duty was that you generally didn't see anyone. Unless you happened to coincide with one of your colleagues on arrival at the store, you didn't see any of them, and the courses weren't yet open so there were no golfers around either. Or, if there were, they were just trying to avoid payment and could therefore be treated with contempt, which I took full advantage of one day as I took great pleasure in flicking one group's balls off the green as I meticulously prepared the course for the paying public. If only I'd been that meticulous that first day…

When I turned up on the Monday morning, I was whisked into a corner of the shed by the chargehand, Billy. "See you, ya wee c★★t, what were you playing at on Saturday?"

It turned out that the phone lines had been red hot on the Saturday with golfer's complaints about the state of the greens on the Burnside and he'd had to come down later and switch them himself. He wasn't overly impressed by my heartfelt pleas that they hadn't looked like they needed it, though I think he eventually accepted my explanation that the eighteenth had been OK and I had simply assumed they were all the same. Maybe the fact I'd done the job properly on the Sunday helped my case, but in any event I only got a metaphorical arse-kicking, which was lucky as Billy had a reputation as a hands-on disciplinarian should the need arise. I must've been forgiven though as I did get another couple of weekends to do that summer. It was, however, a lesson well and truly learned, and I didn't try to shortcut the task ever again.

My only previous experience of the golf course – other than falling in the burn, remember? – had been to record the winning score in an impromptu game of "let's play the last hole of the world-famous Championship Course by kicking a golf ball from the tee to the hole" that a few of us had engaged in late one evening, after all of the golfers had left the course, a couple of years previous. That took something like 23 kicks, which wisnae too shabby considering the fading light and the fact that baseball boots aren't the best surface with which to strike a golf ball!

I'd never shown much interest in golf really – I'd hit a few balls now and again with my brother's old clubs, but I'd never actually played properly – but working on the golf course was potentially a very interesting job. Potentially. Fresh air, peace and quiet, and a variety of relatively unhurried physical tasks to be undertaken, as well as a bit of tractor driving and general skiving. But the Head Greenkeeper, John – the gaffer – had a limited understanding of, and affinity with, the concept of keeping things fresh. No, he had the men who were allocated the grass cutting every day, the men who were allocated the "cupping" every day, and Billy, who pretty much got to do whatever he fancied, so his remit ticked the variety box even if ours didn't.

I was on the cupping team from day one. All day, every day. Well, after 9 a.m. at least. Our first duty each morning was to go round all three courses in teams raking the bunkers – the grass cutters switched the greens and tees before they cut them. Raking was OK, if a wee bit boring, but, even in summer, the north-east coast of Scotland throws up some pretty cold and generally damp weather. Which meant we were always soaked by the time we returned to the shed, even if we wore the waterproofs provided. No moisture-wicking nanotechnology back then, just big, thick yellow plastic waders and sou'westers. The sweat you worked up wearing them soaked you from the inside, and if you left them off then the rain, mist or drizzle soaked you from the outside.

By the time we were finishing the sun would normally be peeking through and you could literally see the steam rising off us as we traipsed back to the shed for our morning break.

By the time 9 a.m. rolled around it was piecie-time, but not until the gaffer declared, "Well, I suppose we can have our piece now."

John was probably just a couple of years shy of retirement then and, to my young and, shamefully, disrespectful eyes, he looked remarkably like Clement Feud. Or actually even more like his dog, Henry the bloodhound.

Nobody dared touch their flask until he uttered those words, yet he did it every day and they all waited. Men of his own vintage, who'd been there as long as he had, but still they waited.

One of the old boys, Jock, had been a clubmaker in St Andrews to trade and had only gone to Carnoustie Golf Course for a week to help a friend out at the Open Championship 40 years before, and he was still there!

It was an extremely strange setting, in the "buckie" as we called it. Being a modern building (it had been built in preparation for the last Open in 1975) the entire shed was functional but completely soulless, and the buckie was no exception. It was probably about three-metre square with white-painted walls, pale grey lino tiles on the floor, polystyrene ceiling tiles and that omnipresent 1970s fluorescent strip lighting that usually had at least one tube on the blink, literally. I think there were windows, but if there were they were high-level narrow things which let in some light but prevented us from seeing anything except a glimpse of sky.

The gaffer's desk was in the centre at the front of the room, and the only other furniture was the 20 or so plastic chairs lined up along the three walls that John could see from his command centre.

I don't think I ever saw John anywhere except in that chair. He was there as we straggled in before 6.30 a.m., turning over his right shoulder to greet each of us individually with a grunted "aye" as we came in, when we came back for piecie-time, when we came back to be dismissed for lunch, when we returned after lunch, and when we came back just before 3.30 p.m. waiting to be officially "loused". The only change in this routine was on a Friday, when we each got called forward individually to collect our wages. And, most of the time, nobody spoke in that room. No joking, no "what did you get up to last night?", nothing – it was quite surreal.

However, if the raking was boring, it was only getting us warmed up in preparation for the cupping. I'll put you out of your misery. Cupping involves, or involved, tying a plastic bucket filled with a soil and seed mixture around your neck and wandering across the fairways dropping handfuls of the mix into the divot holes left from iron shots, and stamping it in. So the technique was set – wander, cup, toss, stamp... and repeat. Ad infinitum!

Honestly, it didn't take long before that degree of tedium really started to get to you. And there wasn't much to distract us apart from the odd passing golfer, but we had to stay out of their way anyway. We were spread out to ensure adequate coverage and, because of the nature of the game, couldn't really shout to each other in case we disturbed the golfers. So the only conversation came when you happened to briefly come into each other's zones, or during the many smoke breaks that one of the old boys, inevitably Jock, would declare. Even if you didn't smoke, as I didn't, you gratefully accepted each opportunity to shed the bucket, lie on the grass or shelter under a tree, depending on the weather, and engage in some banter.

I learned a lot about people and life that summer. Well, you had plenty of time to think given the almost total lack of distraction and the trance-inducing effects of cupping! Even – actually especially – the early morning raking routine was an opportunity to contemplate the meaning of life. Basically, it was a walk in the park, literally, with the occasional bout of raking thrown in. No golfers, no colleagues close by, just two hours of walking, raking and thinking. I can vividly remember looking up at my home town slowly awakening, or across the sea if we happened to be on that side, and basically wondering "what's it all about?"

I guess it would be an entirely different experience now, with an iPhone or iPod to break the monotony, but then it was just me and nature, and a rake. For two hours. Every. Day.

Any deeply philosophical thoughts would inevitably be quickly overtaken by fantasising about how exactly I was going to get closer to any of two or three girls who were currently on my radar. Shallow, *moi*? But even that distraction would eventually be overtaken by the lure of the piecie-break, and the anticipation of finally resolving the growing hunger pangs caused by all of this fresh air and exercise.

Piecie-time was, as I said earlier, a rather sombre affair. Everyone was gathered around the periphery of that basically furnished room, and conversation was awkward. Not that I would've started a conversation anyway. From being one of the pack leaders at school I was firmly back down at the bottom of the pile as "the laddie" who could only really speak when spoken to. It was intimidating, but at least I was gently treated in comparison with the other 17-year-old, Kevin. You see I was a student, technically at least, while Kevin was a bona fide apprentice and therefore fair game to be the butt of whatever cruel humour any of them could dream up. Naturally, when the opportunity arose, I would join in, but seldom in that room.

Kevin was OK actually, a bit gullible and naïve, but basically sound. He used to tow me up the road with his motorbike at lunchtime, me on my racer bike hanging on to his sleeve and managing about 30 miles per hour uphill – don't try this at home, kids!

When we were out cupping (yawn), old Jock used to tease him mercilessly about his (non) sex life. Again, I would join in with this primarily to keep any such spotlight off myself. Jock would say the crudest things to him, which were absolutely hilarious to my ears, of course. He would compare grassy divots to female genitalia and invite Kevin to shut his eyes and feel, for practice! Or he would tell him to "get it while you're young", reminiscing that he used to have six inches and one wrinkle while now he only had six wrinkles and one inch! Those are just two of those kind of stories that stick in my mind.

Other temps who weren't students would also show up.

There was Stan, a strange lad from Dundee who was always late because he was at the mercy of the first bus to Carnoustie. Occasionally he would drive down in his converted ambulance! Never did get to the bottom of that.

My abiding memory of Stan was from a cupping session on the eighteenth fairway of the Burnside. When we spotted golfers approaching, we had to yield to them and stand still quietly until they had played their shots. If we were in their eyeline we were not to move, and we had to be quiet whenever they were in earshot. Usually, we would also retreat to the relative safety of the rough as, in theory, the likelihood was that their shot would land somewhere on the fairway.

Anyway, this day we retreated to the rough and I was just idly looking around as we waited for the all-clear. My eyes fell on Stan about 50 yards away from me on the opposite side of the fairway, and he was equally idly looking up towards the town. A mere second after I caught sight of him he doubled up, fell like a stone and let out an almighty howl as a golf ball caught him square in the abdomen while travelling at considerable pace. Naturally the comic effect of this far outweighed any sympathy or concern for his welfare as the rest of us just fell about laughing. There but for the grace, after all.

Johnny was another temp who arrived, and the only one I could talk football with. Mike was a bit different – he was a good laugh – but he definitely had an edge and I was always a bit wary. Dave was a student who had been there for the previous four summers, an excellent golfer but a very quiet and studious lad who kept himself to himself and didn't really mix. And that was pretty much that as far as young blood was concerned. The two guys who cut the greens were probably in their 40s, but were both Jehovah's Witnesses and didn't mix much either. All the rest, apart from Billy, were getting on for retirement.

Sadly, one of them didn't make it and this led to another one of my reflective periods.

Old Stan, as opposed to temp Stan, had worked at the course for years and was a nice old guy. He didn't often get assigned to cupping, but we worked together a few times, and I used to leave work with him and a few others. He lived very close to the course, only five minutes' walk, so when we headed for home he turned off about a hundred yards after we'd crossed the railway. If you're familiar with the geography of Carnoustie this'll all make sense and if not, visualise.

Anyway, one day I had been working with him all day and as we said, "See you tomorrow," I think we'd been talking about Wimbledon or something. When I got into work the next morning the mood was even more sombre than usual as everyone digested the news that Stan had passed away. Apparently, he got home and sat down to have forty winks, as was his usual routine, but never woke up. He must've died before I'd even reached home. This had a great effect on me and led to even more intensive soul-searching during the raking and cupping tedium.

As you've probably worked out by now, I had never been one for rushing things, but I eventually got round to only my second ever "asking a girl out" phone call that summer. This was another slow burner, in the style that had clearly become my trademark.

I'd been tracking her progress for more than a couple of years since I first spotted her at one of the Monifieth discos and plucked up the courage to dance with her. Frances had been wearing a T-shirt emblazoned with "WANTED" so, summoning all my reserves of cool nonchalance, I asked her what she was wanted for. "Rape," was her laughingly delivered reply! OK then, fair enough… It's a sign of the changing times that such flippant use of language didn't mean then what it would be taken to mean now.

Anyway, my detective work on returning to school resulted in the discovery that she may well be a pretty wee thing, with an intriguing chat-up style, but she was about three years younger than me. I was also, at that time, still going through the whole on–off-on thing with Sheena, so I just maintained my interest at a distance – there was also the small matter that they were both excellent hockey players and knew each other!

Now, in the summer of '77, Frances was still three years younger than me but we were both now also three years older so, finally, I judged that the moment had arrived. Again, I was amazed at how easy the phone call was and how natural the conversation was. Unfortunately, this time around my timing proved to be completely off as she was actually going out with someone at the time. Obviously my tracking hadn't been detailed enough or I would've known this and not made my approach.

To her credit she let me down gently and I could retreat, with dignity, to lick my wounds.

There was nothing else happening on the romance front, so our evening activities continued to focus on generally hanging out, mainly in Monifieth as that's where most of our merry group lived. Weekends were different as we sought out different hostelries, but our dynamic was changing, slowly and almost imperceptibly, probably due to the fact that we no longer saw each other every day and were all experiencing different things in our temporary jobs.

At some point quite early on in the summer, I had decided that I would be needing a rest before starting university in October, what with all this early-start stuff and everything. And, being a fan of round numbers, I concluded that I needed a whole month to prepare myself. Most of the guys kept working and, in hindsight, I should've too as an extra month's money would never have gone amiss. But the wee boy in me needed his holiday so that's what he was going to get. Oh the luxury of long lie-ins again!

Apart from sleeping, I'm not sure what other preparation I did but, ready or not, October rolled around and I was officially a student.

Now, I would generally be inclined to be quite flippant about this, as with most things, but the last few years have generated a fair amount of introspection and revisionism within me, so I'll try to look at this with my sensible head on. This was genuinely a big moment for me and for my family. To my eternal discredit I had no such awareness at the time. But it was.

Despite the expansion in higher education that had taken place in the 1970s, going to university was still a big deal. Probably because it had always been expected of me, it wasn't presented as significant in our household, but it was. I was the first of our family, no matter how widely you cast that definition, to go to university, and I think it's only now that I realise how privileged that made me and how proud it made my family. In 1977 only around 10% of school leavers went to university compared with around 40% nowadays. When my parents were growing up, it would have been closer to 5% so they obviously would rate my going to university as a massive achievement. If only I'd realised, if only I'd understood, if only I'd learned my lessons…

Despite the fact I had just spectacularly failed in my CSYS Mathematics and Chemistry, what did I choose as my subjects for first year at university? Yep, you got it, Mathematics and Chemistry.

I suppose it was inevitable given the drift I was carried along on.

Apart from specifically shying away from electronics, I had given no real thought as to what I wanted to do with my life. Other than play football, of course. And as the notion of any university degree as a general education was still a valid proposition, there was no great pressure to decide on anything concrete. In fact, if anything, choosing Mathematics was all part of this unrecognised and unintentional master plan, as it was generally recognised that a Mathematics degree provided a sound intellectual basis for moving into virtually anything that took your fancy after graduation.

To an extent this still remains the case but it really was true back then. Only, my selection wasn't based on such sound reasoning or indeed any reasoning at all. No, I was just doing what was familiar and what I had previously been good at. Even if I'd slowly been demonstrating that the more familiar I became, the lower my achievements became.

So, my first-year programme became Pure Mathematics, Applied Mathematics and Chemistry. Due to the innovative, at that time, modular structure of courses at the University of Dundee, only one other student in the whole of first year followed an identical course, a funny-looking wee girl that I don't think I ever spoke to, not even once. Well, she looked funny to me, and not in a good way. I don't suppose she rated me highly either, especially as I never spoke to her.

The Pure Mathematics course introduced me to another of that select band of major influences in my life, the one and only Dr Charlie Dixon. Charlie was brilliant, a great mathematician and a great people person − a rare combination, believe me. He was so enthusiastic and would rattle around the blackboard at great speed saying everything twice while writing it once then stopping to check if we were with him. Whether we were or not we were never going to tell him, but at least he asked.

If you went to see him privately, he could explain the topic in as many ways as it took, progressively coming down until he determined your current level of understanding before patiently building you up again. And all with a smile on his face.

Charlie was about five feet tall and was into curling and playing the bagpipes, though not at the same time, obviously. What a character. I will never forget all he did for me and, sincerely, thanks, Charlie.

His sidekick was Dr Hamish Anderson, a kindly old soul who was very gentle but didn't have Charlie's ability to connect with everyone at every level. His outstanding feature was continually referring to mathematical variables as beasties or creatures. Hamish and Charlie were great pals, and both took their responsibilities towards their students a lot more seriously than we were taking our responsibilities towards our studies!

Applied Mathematics was split into three different topics across each of the three terms. Term 1 was Computing, a radically different beastie (thanks, Hamish) then than now, and we all used to write BASIC or ALGOL programs to solve simple problems and tap into the mainframe at UMIST in Manchester for more complex stuff. Hard to believe but I've probably got more computing power in my iPhone than existed then in the whole university, UMIST included!

Term 2 was Statistics and Probability, and Term 3 was Mechanics. I hated that – it was way too close to Physics for my liking and I'd long since given up on that.

Chemistry was my chance to meet up with my thwarted GP amigos who were finally getting to do three sciences in one year. In case you're wondering what happened to my Pharmacology ambitions – well, my gran needn't have worried about farming after all as I'd completely binned that idea some time ago, no doubt seduced by the aesthetic beauty of the one pure science. When I later heard tales of having to kill baby chicks for biological experimentation, I knew I'd made the right decision.

There were a couple of strange rituals of uni life that are probably worth recalling here, one formal and one much more informal.

Conjuring up images more akin to something out of *Porterhouse Blue*, the University of Dundee operated a Regent system whereby each fresher, or first-year entrant, was allocated to a senior member of the academic staff for mentoring and support, along with three or four other students. My Regent, Dave Thomas, happened to also be my Applied Mathematics lecturer, which actually made the formality of it even more awkward.

His initial contribution to my social and academic development came in the form of an invitation to dinner with him and his wife at their home, accompanied by my fellow whatever-we-were-calleds. Now, on the one hand this was a lovely gesture and involved a lot of work, mostly by Dave's no doubt long-suffering wife, who had to prepare a meal for a group of reluctant and, probably, ungrateful youths every year. On the other... it was torture! Well meaning, but torture.

We sat around the formal dining table, eating politely and only really speaking when spoken to – none of us students knew each other. Apart from all being at the University of Dundee, and having Dave as our Regent, we had nothing in common. It was a long and painful evening, and with apologies to Mrs Thomas in particular, the best bit was when we were able to leave. I don't recall who the other students were – I don't think I ever saw any of them, even from a distance, again, and I can't remember any other attempts at regenting being made after that. All in all, just an elitist, ceremonial box-ticking exercise.

The other ritual – which all universities have a version of, I think – was Gaudie Night, followed a month later by Raisin Monday. Gaudie Night was held on the Friday at the end of the first week and involved being adopted by some senior students and treated to a tour of some local haunts. Al, Jimmy and I were picked up by a couple of second-year girls and, after an introductory drink in the Union, headed off to visit a few establishments on the Perth Road.

To be fair, we didn't drink that much over the course of the evening but, at our final pub, our drinks were definitely spiked by some male friends of the girls. Boy, were we ill

– Jimmy, especially, was virtually comatose! I've no idea how we all got home, though I vaguely think one of the girls drove us, but I do clearly remember sleeping with a basin beside my bed!

The reciprocal event was Raisin Monday, traditionally the first Monday in November, when we would meet up again with the students who had taken us out and return the favour. We did, but I think we were a lot more careful, and I'm sure I remember the two girls being a wee bit sheepish when we met up.

The academic year started off alright, probably because it was all new. I used to meet up with my old schoolmates every lunchtime in the Student Union, where we'd have ferocious table tennis sessions in the basement or the occasional more laid-back game of snooker upstairs. Lunch was usually the bargain Ploughman's – 30p! – washed down with a carton of pineapple juice or milk. Oh the high life! But a whole carton of pineapple juice? Up until this point in my life pineapple juice, like orange or grapefruit, was only ever served up in thimble-sized glasses in hotels at breakfast time.

Despite overdosing regularly on fruit juice, I was struggling with the subjects, but not so much that I actually realised it at this stage. I thought that I'd learned that I really did have to study, but my version of that was to religiously copy out all of my notes again each night. Obsessively neat, underlined and colour-coded, they remain instantly accessible. But I had fallen into the classic didactic learning model trap, where the notes of the lecturer become the notes of the student without passing through the minds of either. Of course, I didn't realise that was the case until many years later, but that's exactly what was going on.

I still retained some kind of blind faith that everything would come good, but the writing was on the wall from quite early on. Increasingly, I just wasn't enjoying myself and completely unconsciously simply retreated into my shell. I would turn up, mostly, listen and copy notes, play table tennis, listen and copy more notes, go home, and copy the copied notes more neatly, then go to bed. From Monday through Friday I had no life, and no enjoyment.

At the weekend I would spring back into life, go out with friends, go to the football with Dad, play football, and to the outside world, indeed even to my family, I would've appeared to be a happy-go-lucky, carefree young student. Except that I wasn't, I was really toiling, and when we reached the end-of-year exams, and the inevitable happened, I was at crisis point. I didn't want to keep going, because I knew within myself that I couldn't. The only real problem with that thought was that I still hadn't a clue what I wanted to do instead. But some level of maturity must've been kicking in at last, as I resolved to put all my efforts into the September resits, then decide what to do next from there.

So, I turned up for that year's council summer job interview looking forward to the mental escape from what had turned out to be, for me, academic torture. The pattern could be ignored no longer – straight A, straight B, straight D, complete meltdown! So any kind of repetitive, unthinking, physical job in the fresh air had to be just the tonic required, preferably just not one with a 6.30 a.m. start if you don't mind.

The Head of Angus Council's Parks Department said that John, the Head Greenkeeper, would be disappointed that I wasn't to be returning but that he was happy to offer me the job I'd originally wanted with the Parks and Cemeteries crew. As that started at a much more acceptable 8 a.m., I gratefully accepted. My soft side resurfaced though, and I did experience more than a few twangs of regret about the golf course, especially now that I'd been told they had wanted me back. It's always good to feel wanted, but it must be significant that, even having achieved the outcome that I wanted, the guilt of letting people down would haunt me for the next wee while.

Turning up on the first day anywhere is always nerve-wracking, especially for me, as I was beginning to recognise myself, but there were lots of similarities between the organisation at the council yard and what I'd experienced the year before at the golf course. The room we gathered in was a lot smaller, mind, and the chairs and, well, everything really, were absolutely minging, but there was the same general arrangement. Everyone strolled in, grunted some form of greeting, and sat in silence awaiting the word.

One difference was that the gaffer, Geordie, had a separate office, shed actually, and his chargehand, Jim, would be across there receiving the instructions for the day before coming to get us. Then we would load all the necessary equipment for the day onto a trailer or into the back of the van, before we got loaded into the back of the van too and transported off to whichever part of Carnoustie was in urgent need of our attention.

I spent the first day, the first three days actually, doing nothing but edging grass in the gardens of a housing scheme. Suddenly cupping didn't seem quite so bad. At least I never got injured with cupping – I was clearly gripping the edging shears too tightly, to the extent that when I returned home on day one my forearms were absolutely solid! The next morning I had to soak my hands and arms in hot water to try to loosen them into usability, only to top up the agony with another eight-hour edging stint.

After day three I plucked up the courage to complain about this, and was promoted to grass cutting. Now this I enjoyed. Apart from the noise, which I diluted by sticking cotton wool in my ears.

There was, and is, something therapeutic about cutting grass. I like the straight lines, and the instantly obvious transformation from long to short. I'd found my gardening mojo! I wasn't so keen on raking up afterwards though, which we sometimes had to do, especially if the grass was very long. But cutting grass provided an opportunity to get back inside your own head, insulated from the outside world by the noise and earplugs, and just think. That wasn't always a good thing for me, as we've already established several times over, but the agonising over "what happens next" was something that I really had to do, and this provided the perfect opportunity to do so.

I had hoped that this job would provide variety, compared with the golf course, and it certainly did to some extent. Whereas the golf course duties could be summarised as raking, cupping, mixing soil and seed when it rained, and sometimes filling the washer bottles on a Friday, there was a much more extensive menu with the Parks Department. The good: grass cutting, hedge trimming, marking football pitches. The bad: hoeing and weeding, edging, raking. And the ugly: anything involving Shanwell Cemetery! My heart would just sink when I knew we were heading for the cemetery. You knew it was coming too, as we would never go more than two weeks without returning. I just kept hoping that I would be dropped off somewhere else that day, to finish off in a housing scheme, or to help Chic at the bowling green, or anything other than go there.

In terms of being in a confined space it was far worse than the golf course. There, you had distance and horizons; at the cemetery you could see the walls. And the gravestones. Lots of them. Nothing else, no people or passing traffic, or noise or any other distraction. The grass cutting was awkward too as you had to go up and down each individual grave. That meant there were literally miles of edges, so no escape from edging, and loads of hoeing and weeding too. All... In... Silence...

Occasionally we'd be there when a funeral was taking place, and we'd respectfully retreat behind the van until the ceremony was over and the mourners had left. That was a bit spooky, though not as bad as the time I was promoted to assist in the filling-in of a grave. I think there were two funerals at the same time, one at Barry and one at Shanwell. There were four guys in the crew who were the designated gravediggers, and I think one of them was off so... take a step forward, Cadet Craigie.

I think it was a compliment, showing that I had earned their trust, but it was one never repeated after I inadvertently threw a shovelful of earth straight into Chic's coupon! He was in the grave stamping the earth down − I know − and I was shovelling the earth in, trying hard not to think too much about what I was doing. I must've been distracting myself successfully as, on one swoosh, I hadn't noticed that Chic had moved from the far end to my end and so he duly received a mouthful of sandy soil for his troubles. I got a good shouting at, though he accepted it was an accident, and I never got selected for grave duties again. Result!

Seriously, I admired the job the gravediggers did. Their way of coping was to see it as a hole and a box, and not get emotionally involved in any way. They were generally respectful, though I do recall with horror one story they told of discovering a set of false teeth at the side of a grave after they'd already filled it in! They reckoned they must've dug them up, from the previous resident, then not noticed. And apparently going through the box, as in putting your foot through the coffin, was a common occurrence, especially with old graves...

On the personal front, something else happened during this summer though, something quite sinister that I still don't understand to this day.

One evening, with no entertainment planned, I jumped on my bike and headed off towards Monifieth thinking I would see Baz and generally just hang out. I didn't phone first as I didn't explicitly know that's what I was going to do when I first went out, but it was a nice evening, so what the hell.

On reaching Monifieth, as I cycled past one of the streets where one of our peripheral group members lived, I noticed the rest of our squad hanging around outside his house. Baz was there, and Al, Jimmy, all of them actually. My instinct, which I will never understand or be able to explain, was not to swing by and say, "Hi, guys, what's happening," and announce my unscheduled arrival, but instead to immediately head home feeling somehow snubbed.

I know this makes no sense. How could I be snubbed? They didn't even know I was planning on being there. But snubbed I felt and I instantly resolved that the next contact should be from one of them. I fully expected Baz to phone me within a couple of days, not to check that I was alright, as he had no way of knowing there was any reason or even non-reason for me not being alright, but just routinely as he had done for the previous three years. Except that phone call never came – ever. I have never heard from him again, nor any of the others. Why, I have no idea, but if I initially thought that I'd been snubbed, I knew I definitely had now! Big time.

What went wrong? I genuinely don't know. Baz and I had been really close for three years. The last time I can recall speaking to him on the phone before all this, whatever "this" was, happened, I remember he was unimpressed that I'd been out with a girl that he didn't rate, but it was a nothing conversation really. What had it got to do with him, and what was there for him to be unimpressed about anyway? She was a nice girl, but we only went out three, or maybe four, times over a period of a couple of weeks before she mutually agreed that we should stop! I wasn't all loved up or otherwise distracted, so I was still the same as I'd always been. I have no idea what happened.

Anyway, not for the last time, I had concluded that friendship was only genuine and worthwhile if it was reciprocal and that maybe I had been the one putting in all the effort. After all, for three years I had been in Monifieth practically every night – had any of those guys been in Carnoustie, other than for school? Was it me who phoned all the time? Jeez, this sounds like the analysis of a love affair gone wrong and I suppose, in a way, it was. But whatever happened, in their minds, for me that summer signalled the end of an era and there would be no going back.

A more memorable event, for all the right reasons this time, happened towards the end of that summer when I was headhunted to represent Carnoustie in the Angus Sportstown '78 competition – granted, it wisnae the Olympics, but it was still fairly exciting stuff for our sleepy wee corner of the county.

One of my former PE teachers, and future friend and colleague, John Fletcher, contacted me to ask if I would like to be part of the volleyball team and also his partner in a football dribble relay. Football and volleyball, what's not to like, so I was happy to accept.

I remember panicking a little bit about what to wear, and actually went and bought my first ever tracksuit the day before, a splendid adidas number consisting of a red zippered top with the iconic three black stripes and black bottoms with red stripes – tangerine wasn't available, at least not in my price range!

Anyway, we headed up to Forfar Leisure Centre on a mid-September Sunday for the nine-hour competition which involved six team sports – badminton, table tennis, hockey, netball, basketball and volleyball, and also three dribbling relays in football, hockey and basketball. Well, our team was just unstoppable, winning just about every individual event comfortably and finishing with 300 points – 130 ahead of Forfar, with Arbroath, Brechin and Montrose even further behind. Not too shabby for the smallest town in the competition...

Somewhere, somehow, during all this fun and frolics, I had concluded that I would do the resit exams, but I definitely wasn't going back to uni. Although I still didn't know what I wanted to do, I was definite that I couldn't continue as I was, but that passing the resits would help to keep my options open. I actually managed to study quite well for those exams – needs must and all that – and managed to pass them quite comfortably. That wasn't enough to change my mind though – I just looked on that as mission accomplished. There was to be no early finish from the summer job this year either, and I stayed on until they eventually chucked me out at the start of October. Everyone else I knew headed back to uni, and I headed... into the unknown.

CHAPTER 9

... and drifting right back out again!

(1978-1979)

And so it began. My year out. My gap year. Nothing unusual in that – nowadays. Back then it would've been revolutionary, but it wasn't. I was ahead of the curve, except I wasn't. No, however much a gap year can be painted as an opportunity to grow and develop, a year off the treadmill to take stock, part of a master plan to help you become a much more rounded individual... if I was to seriously claim any of that was in my mind then I'd be deluding myself. All I knew was that I didn't want another year like I'd just had. Whatever confidence I'd had in my academic ability had faded to almost nothing. The straight A student, the dux, hadn't completely left the building completely though – I just knew that the path I'd stumbled upon, more than chosen, was not for me. But what to do?

My plan, such as it was, was to have a damn good think and, amazingly, my parents went along with this. I say amazingly but that's unfair as my parents were always incredibly supportive and just wanted their wee boy to be happy. They'd almost certainly have preferred it if I was powering through uni en route to a steady, well-paid career, but they never really showed that. Instead, they seemed to accept that I was a crazy, mixed-up kid who needed some time to figure things out. Not for the first or the last time, thanks, folks.

So, instead of heading back to the world of academia, mid-October saw me heading off on holiday with Mum and Dad to a little cottage in the countryside near Forres in Morayshire. If nothing else that holiday has left me with one of my most treasured photos of my mum, being cuddled by a remarkably young, shiny, good-looking, smiling, long-haired youth resplendent in red jumper and very wide flares.

Apart from the photo, the only other details of the holiday that I can remember are going out for a run very early on our first day there, and Mum complaining that the place had fleas! The run I recall because it was freezing that morning. Literally, very frosty and slippy. So much so that it was not to be repeated. As for the fleas, well we'd loaded the car up with our own bedding, but I think Ma and Pa slept on the settee after the first night as she was convinced she'd been bitten. She always claimed she had delicate skin, a quality which, unfortunately, I've inherited. I think we were meant to be there a week but probably called it quits after five days.

Returning home meant embarking on a remarkable period with nothing specific to do. While doing all this soul-searching and career planning, my intention was to get a job to earn my keep. After signing on at the buroo in Arbroath, I was committed to returning every fortnight until gainful employment was sourced. As I was only really interested in doing something in Carnoustie, this meant the net was not being cast very wide. The Job Centre only came up with one suggestion during the entire period, while my scouring of the newspapers only yielded two.

First up, postman. I really fancied this as it struck me as being very like my summer jobs had been, in that you got exercise and fresh air while not having to think a lot about the task, therefore leaving plenty time for all that thinking I had to do.

Interview acquired, easy-peasy this job-hunting lark, I duly presented myself at Carnoustie's rather grand GPO building one evening around 6 p.m. First up was what could only be described as an IQ test, which I scooshed. Straight A student, remember? That was followed by an interview, which I thought went exceedingly well. The Postmaster commented that they'd never had anyone score as highly on the IQ test, natch, which I took as a very good sign.

He ran through the terms and conditions, hours of work, duties, etc. and enthusiastically detailed the extra 50p a week payable for cleaning your bike like this was a great incentive. Everything sounded good and I left the building convinced that my early starts were about to return and a few months of being a postie was about to kick-off.

I had been very careful during the interview to make it sound like I was interested in a long-term postal career, as I reckoned telling them I only wanted the job for a few months until I returned to uni would not make me an attractive candidate. Unfortunately, they weren't convinced by this and rejected me as being overqualified and unlikely to stay. Accurate, but unfair I thought. The fact they gave the gig to a recently retired (in disgrace) policeman was my first introduction to the real world.

Anyway, I didn't have long to wait for interview number two – as a van driver for a frozen sausage company. Once again, decent interview, everything sounded OK, but the whole "overqualified and unlikely to stay" thing kicked in again and young Gordie was kicked into touch once more.

Never mind – an unexpected phone call from the Job Centre a few days later offered up a great opportunity to be a Range Warden at the Barry Buddon army camp.

Now, again with hindsight, this would've been ideal. Fresh air, exercise, little responsibility etc., etc., ticks all the boxes. Except to me, it just sounded like an excellent opportunity to get shot at or to step on an unexploded bomb and so I, somewhat irrationally I would now accept, rejected the chance of an interview out of hand. While sympathising with the outcomes of the first two interviews, Dad thought I was bonkers to turn this one down though I think Mum shared my fears and so there wasn't too much made of it.

This burst of job-seeking activity must've all happened over the October–December period and the rest of my time was taken up with frequent visits to the University Careers Centre, the library and gathering information about, mainly, sport and physical education courses. Yes, I had long held the thought that I might enjoy being a PE teacher.

I realise this is not entirely unusual amongst sporty boys, but for some reason, I had never really fancied the Scottish route of "going to Jordanhill". I think it was because it seemed a bit elitist and very rugby-orientated, though it may also have been heavily influenced by the fact that I considered most of the people I knew who had gone there to be twats!

Anyway, in those pre-internet days, gathering information meant writing off by snail mail and awaiting replies and so there was a steady stream of prospectuses crashing through our letter box from all manner of obscure English colleges and universities. Quite why a boy who went pale at the prospect of living in Glasgow thought Exeter was ever going to be a goer I don't know, but Exeter, along with the splendidly named Strawberry Hill College in Twickenham, was one of the candidates amongst many, many others.

I even went as far as applying to some, and was certainly accepted for interview at Loughborough which, although I didn't quite realise it then, is really for the crème de la crème of the physical education and sports science world. Rather conveniently, when the interview was scheduled I picked up an ankle injury playing football and therefore couldn't have undertaken the physical tests. By the time the rearranged interview came around, I had finally settled on an alternative plan and so apologetically withdrew. Sliding doors, eh?

Having maintained all the way through this tale that I hadn't a clue what I wanted to do, then suddenly pulling the whole PE teacher thing out of the bag, I should probably explain this a bit more fully.

Apart from when I was very young, when I wanted to be an electrician just like my dad and my brother, the only other thoughts I had ever remotely entertained for any length of time (apart from being a professional footballer) centred on teaching. Dave Fimister had been, and remained, a great inspiration to me and, for a while, being a primary school teacher held some appeal. Teaching a breadth of subjects, taking the football team, influencing young minds – that all sounded quite attractive.

Mum and Dad thought so too, so this was a tentative, almost unspoken, plan when I was around 12–14. Then I fell under the spell of Ed Black and was attracted to his model of being a Mathematics teacher, but by this time I was apparently astute enough to understand that maybe I was just looking at what I knew, what I was familiar with, so it never really developed much beyond an attraction. Besides, it wasn't very cool to aspire to become a teacher while you were at school, not when everybody else around you was desperate to escape the school environment.

The PE teacher thing emerged later on, though there was an unfair stigma attached in that the guys who followed that path weren't always viewed as the brightest.

And then there was football, there was always football, but I'd always genuinely considered that to be something that either would or wouldn't happen naturally and couldn't really be planned for.

Anyway, somewhere in the midst of all this soul-searching, I had an epiphany…

As my gap year progressed, and winter turned to spring, I had finally exhausted all of the possibilities afforded by the University Careers Service. A lovely lady, Barbara Taylor, the head of the service, had patiently and kindly guided me through all kinds of tests and information gathering, and I'd done all sorts of research on my own. My breakthrough came when I finally realised that, once again, I couldn't go on like this and had to come to some conclusion so I could start to move forward again. I concluded that as teaching was the only real occupation that I had ever considered as a serious possibility, then that was what I should do.

My research had confirmed that for primary teaching any degree would do, and in order to qualify as a secondary Mathematics teacher then I would have to have at least two consecutive graduating courses in Mathematics within my degree.

At this point I was clear in my mind what the objective was, teaching, and therefore I knew that an ordinary degree would suffice. I was also sufficiently self-aware to recognise that I didn't have the interest and commitment in Mathematics per se to sustain me through an honours degree but, if that position changed, I could always pick that up later. Therefore, remarkably for me, I had somehow arrived at a very clear and achievable plan – two more years at uni to get a degree containing two graduating courses in Mathematics, followed by one year at teacher training college, then I would be entering the professional job market at exactly the same time as my peers. Sorted. And, in the best Gordie tradition, it also kept my options open – primary teacher, secondary teacher, or anything else that required a general degree!

All of my research meant that I knew the rules and regulations of the university inside out and therefore knew exactly what my options were for course choices and progression. I also knew I could select courses from both the Science and Arts faculties, an option that was specific to Dundee, so my choices were not restricted only to the sciences. Mind you, as we've already ascertained, offering me more choices was not always a good thing!

So, my plan was that for my first year back I would return to the Pure Mathematics course that I should've passed first time around plus two others that interested me in some way, and then the following year I would progress to the follow-on Pure Mathematics course plus one other.

For reasons which I don't recall I had somehow become interested in studying Economics, so that took care of one choice from the Faculty of Arts. Interestingly, I was to be allowed entry into second-year Economics on the grounds that the first-year syllabus would be covered in the first fortnight anyway! This confirmed my long-held suspicions that Arts courses were easier than Science courses! My other choice then became purely pragmatic, even if later on in life it would seem more than a little ironic, and I chose what appeared to be an easy option of Accountancy.

And so, with all of that resolved by the springtime, I was free to make my earliest ever start with the council and return to my lawnmower at the first available opportunity, probably around the end of May. This time though, I didn't have to torture myself with thoughts of "what am I going to do?" and I was able to relax and simply go with the flow. Happy, carefree days – could they last?

They certainly lasted through that summer, in complete contrast to the mental torments of the previous one. I learned a lot about life, and about people, including myself, during those summer stints. The permanent guys were generally quite accepting of whatever young whippersnappers turned up each year to help them, though one or two of them weren't slow to let us know that we weren't as clever as we thought we were – an interesting observation when balanced against some of the stupid things they did. Like whenever the time and motion study man would turn up to time a new job, for the purposes of calculating bonus payments, and our chargehand, Jim, would insist on working twice as fast as usual while he was being timed.

The number of times we tried to explain to him that he was doing us all out of bonuses and setting impossible targets was completely lost on him. Thankfully, his second in command, Chic, was more switched on and would always try to keep Jim away from these timing sessions.

Everyday acts of stupidity, allied to a constant disregard of anything that could possibly be construed as health and safety, were the norm. Such as loading half a dozen men plus a couple of lawnmowers and cans of petrol into the back of a transit van, then half the occupants starting to smoke – those were also the conditions under which, on rainy days, we'd spend piecie-time... Quite why nobody ever caught anything, or got blown up, will always remain a mystery.

There was one hilarious story that comes from that setting, however, on a day when our break was extended because it was raining. Much of our work couldn't really be carried out in the rain, but our genius chargehand would never call a halt to proceedings until we were already soaked.

One such morning he called us all back into the van for an early piecie-break, so with six of us drookit in the back, and the three more senior guys in the front, the steam rising off all nine of us very quickly misted up the front and rear windows.

As we all sat there, breathing in that heady mix of cigarette smoke, petrol fumes, wet grass and drying-out-sweat and grime, the rain continued to batter down on the van roof. Every so often we'd hear Jim's words of wisdom on the weather situation, but nobody could actually see outside. Somehow, we three or four young scoundrels in the back realised that the rain was easing, so we started to take it in turn to rap our nails off the roof to mimic the sound of rainfall – Jim was taken in hook, line and sinker, for over an hour!

After a wee while Chic realised what was happening but, since he didn't want to get wet again either, just smiled at us and we carried on with the scam until Jim announced that we'd be as well heading back to the depot for an early lunch. He still didn't twig when Chic started the van up and flicked the windscreen wipers to reveal, well, no rain – students one, gardeners nil!

One day, while cutting grass in one of the council housing schemes, I walked past a garden and was surprised to see my fellow student Barry lying in the middle of it with his hands over his face and his mower whirring away beside him. I asked him what he was doing and he said, "Gordon, could you please look at my foot? I think I've cut a toe off."

What?

From his tone I could tell he wasn't joking but I could also perfectly well see that his trainer was intact and there was no blood so… there was a high probability that he still had the same number of toes that he had started the day with. So I told him that, probably more concisely and with a few expletives attached, and he opened his eyes and looked for himself, breathed out a quick "Thank God" and proceeded to tell his tale. Apparently, he'd slipped on the damp grass and his foot had gone under the mower – he was so convinced that the blade had sliced through his foot that he was frightened to look.

I hardly ever remind him of that when we reminisce nowadays!

Possibly the same day, certainly in the same housing scheme, I managed to mangle one of those rubber link doormats as I took a shortcut across somebody's front step, and also inadvertently gave another doormat a haircut, having not learned my lesson the first time!

More spectacular was the time when I was sent into the caravan site next to the depot to Flymo under the caravans.

This was not a regular job but carried out periodically when the grass under some of the static vans got too long and unsightly – the required technique was to kind of throw the Flymo under the van a bit to get as far back as you could.

Anyway, on this particular occasion I had failed to see a TV aerial cable lying under the van, and when I threw the Flymo under, the cable wrapped itself around the revolving blade, causing the Flymo to shoot back towards me then out of my hands and onto the roof of the caravan, whereupon it finally choked out the motor and came to rest. Thankfully there was nobody at home and a quick check around suggested there were no witnesses, so I climbed up, untangled my weapon, replaced the cable as best I could and sauntered off innocently.

After Barry's mishap with his training shoes we both became a bit more safety conscious and started wearing the steel-toecapped boots we were supplied with each year. Our first day always involved being asked to supply our shoe size and our chest/waist measurements so we could be supplied with boots, dungarees and a jacket – initially the clothes were regulation navy blue but soon turned to safety orange as health and safety eventually began to be a thing.

On my last summer, the gaffer summoned me to personally collect my boots and clothes – this was unusual as Jim was normally allocated the task of just handing them out. Geordie looked at me a bit suspiciously and said, "This is your fifth year with us, and we've been supplying you with boots for four of them. Your feet have been a different size every time – why is that?"

I could tell there was a wee smile behind the question, so I decided to tell him the truth. "Well, the first year the boots were for me, the second for my dad, last year for my brother and this year, I'm actually needing a new pair."

His smile broadened and he said, "Aye, that's fine. I just wondered."

My absolute favourite job, unsurprisingly, came about each August when we would resurrect all of the football pitches around the town. The goalposts would be moved, literally, to allow for wear and tear on the grass to be evened out, and this also meant that the pitches all had to be freshly marked out with sawdust – old-school!

I was fascinated to discover that they ensured the right angles in the corner by utilising the Theorem of Pythagoras – not that any of the regulars knew that's what they were doing!

Once they decided where the corner was going to be they would stick a metal pin in the ground. Then they would decide on the precise direction of the goal line and place another pin exactly three feet away. The next step was the clever one – the tape measure would be secured under the first pin, and another pin would be wrapped into the tape at the four-feet mark then, with the tape pulled tight, that wrapped-up pin would be scraped across the grass to mark out an arc four feet away from the first pin.

A similar procedure was then carried out from the second pin, but with the wrapped pin at the five-feet mark. The intersection of the two arcs therefore completed the 3:4:5 triangle and, hence, a perfect right angle between goal line and touchline.

A long string would then be stretched out following that line and the sawdust would be laid on top until we reached the 100-yard mark where the whole Pythagoras routine would be played out again – genius!

Two or three years into my tenure, we encountered a problem when the tape measure that Jim had used religiously since the year nineteen oatcake, broke at either the four- or five-feet mark, no doubt suffering from repetitive strain syndrome! With no other tape available there was a hint of panic in the air and much chin-scratching ensued. Your trusty resident mathematician came to the rescue, advising that we could still use the tape but that we'd use 5:12:13 instead – why I didn't suggest sticking with 3:4:5 but just from a different starting point, I have absolutely no idea! – but Jim just looked at me as if I was daft!

I persevered, without actually giving him a trigonometry lesson, but he was having none of it until Chic intervened on my behalf saying, "Jim, the laddie's at university daein Maths – he kens whit he's daein."

Jim still looked suspicious but reluctantly agreed so we went through the usual procedure, but using 5:12:13, and, hey presto, one perfectly marked out football pitch. He still looked at me like I'd performed some kind of witchcraft and a new tape measure appeared in the van the next day so that the good old days of 3:4:5 could be returned to without further delay!

Even going up to the sawmill near Monikie to get fresh sawdust was an adventure, and Chic would always take me. It meant a change of scenery, a hurl in the van, and an hour away from real work, so what's not to like? Maybe he was just trying to make up for the first time he took me up, when he told me to stand underneath the hopper and catch the sawdust in a sack – you're probably ahead of me now, reader. Some of the sawdust did indeed go straight into the sack, but by far the greater portion simply engulfed the naïve fool standing directly below it! Or maybe that was just his revenge for the gravedigging episode...

When I think back to those summers, I do think of them fondly. Some days I could've seen it all far enough, especially when it was raining and miserable – or when we were in Shanwell – but the overall impact on my life was overwhelmingly positive. Manual labour, mixing with men I would never have met under different circumstances, and having time to just think about something or nothing while repetitively pushing a mower around – all of that was worthwhile, and the money was good too, for a student job. It also means I can pull out the "I was once a professional gardener" line any time it suits me, though that doesn't sit well with my wife when she's moaning about the state of our garden! Ach, cobbler's bairns...

CHAPTER 10

Return of the prodigal

(1979–1982)

Here we go then, student life, take two!

The timetable afforded by my combination of Pure Mathematics, Accountancy and Economics was very favourable and meant I could once again get a lift to Dundee from my dad and have plenty time to get to wherever I needed to get to. My crossover into the Arts and Social Sciences faculty, through Economics, introduced me to the concept of tutorials, where small groups got together and discussed the topics of the week, a stark contrast to science labs and even Mathematics tutorials which exclusively consisted of slogging through lots of hard sums.

Accountancy, initially at least, was proving to be every bit as easy as I'd hoped, and with my new-found resolve and determination, Applied Mathematics seemed more straightforward this time, and my love of Mathematics appeared to be returning. I also decided to take advantage of some of the other university facilities and started going to the gym three times a week to lift weights, something I'd wanted to do for a while but had never got around to.

My experience was seemingly altogether different this time around. Yes, I was older and wiser, by a whole year (?), but I think the main difference was that I now had a purpose. I had made a definite decision to do this based on sound reasoning. My goals were clear and I was now motivated. I was back in a happy place, and everything was going smoothly.

I acquired new friends – Neil, in Mathematics, and Elizabeth, in Economics. She was purely a study buddy, as I think I only ever saw her once outwith the lecture theatre, but we always sat together if we could and just had a laugh. She was blonde, English and bubbly, and totally different to every other girl I had previously met at uni. Although she was clearly bright, she wasn't in any way stuffy or serious and I think we just mutually helped each other through that course.

Neil was a bit of a budding Mathematics and Physics genius, but he was seriously musical too. We hung out a lot, played a bit of snooker, and even entertained thoughts of hooking up musically with me singing and him playing guitar. That kind of fell apart when we realised that, although I could sing a bit, I appeared to lose any ability that I had as soon as he started strumming. He would get exasperated, telling me that he would follow me, but I could never quite get that. Besides, I would never have been able to sing in public – what were we thinking?

Mind you, I did have a track record, which I forgot to mention earlier – somewhere in the S4/S5 years, so around 1975/6, I had been the frontman for a three-piece rock band... OK, if I left it there that would definitely be classified as being economical with the truth! Back then, Stooge had been getting into playing guitar and Barry McCormack, the only drummer we knew, moved his entire drum kit into Stooge's bedroom so that they could practise together. Soon enough it was agreed that I should be the singer to help (?) them struggle their way through "All Right Now" and "Panic in Detroit" which, as I hazily recall, constituted our entire repertoire – rock and roll, eh?

This time around, knowing the rules inside out meant fully understanding that good performances in the first two sets of term exams meant exemption from the year exam. So, with that as an added incentive, I blitzed through the term exams! Nothing if not pragmatic, me. Especially as far as Accountancy was concerned.

Term 1 had consisted of some basic principles and some computing, so far so good, but Term 2 introduced some actual accounting, balance sheets and the like. Now, the principle of this is incredibly simple, but in practice I simply could not get to grips with putting things in somewhere only to take them out elsewhere. It all seemed unnecessarily complicated, ridiculous and a little labyrinthine, and my brain rebelled against it.

When the term exam came around there was a section on stocks and shares, which I aced, a multiple-choice section, which again I aced, apart from any of the balance sheet questions, and a balance sheet section in which I scrambled through with the bare minimum. And that, dear reader, is how I managed to acquire a graduating course in Accountancy without ever understanding the whys and wherefores of balancing accounts.

In all probability this is where my distrust and dislike of the entire Accountancy profession began. What a lot of bollocks! A totally made up profession, in my humble opinion, where they have shamelessly made up their own rules and, along with lawyers (don't get me started!), enshrined these in law so that the rest of us have to fall into line while paying them vast sums of money to satisfy these rules. If I need any further justification for my long-standing hatred I only have to consider the financial crisis caused by the bankers, politicians and accountants, and I rest my case.

Anyway, cruising through the term exams left me *finito* by around the middle of May and ready to return to my grass-cutting career once again. What a completely different feeling though, heading into five months of freedom, when everything is going right for a change!

However, after a memorable summer, to which we will return later, it was eyes down, look in once more for what was scheduled to be my final year.

Pure Mathematics and Economics were both a given and, against my better judgement, I was persuaded that progressing in Applied Mathematics would be a good idea too.

That didn't last too long. The first couple of weeks went well enough as simple probability and statistics is quite interesting and quite easy. Dr Terry Brown made a monumental mistake early on however when he told us that if we bought the textbook – which he had written – then we didn't really have to come to the lectures.

Now, this is bad on two counts. One, unabashed and gratuitous salesmanship from which he must benefit commercially. Two, what an indictment of lectures as purely a transmission model of learning. The notes of the lecturer become the notes of the student without passing through the minds of either. Again.

The death knell for his course came one lunchtime when Neil and I made the mistake of turning up too early for his lecture. As we slumped on the vinyl sofas outside the lecture theatre watching the clock tick slowly around to 2 p.m. we discussed the merits of Applied Mathematics. Five minutes later we had concluded that neither of us enjoyed the course, neither of us needed the course, and that we would both benefit from dropping it. And with that, as our classmates arrived and started filing in, we left and never returned.

One of the upsides of this radical move was the vastly reduced workload. This left plenty of time to reschedule my gym sessions to the morning before progressing to Pure Mathematics, lunch, Economics, then home. More precisely, Dad would drop me off around 9.30 a.m. in the West Port, just around the corner from his work. I would stroll onto campus to reach the gym for opening time, 10 a.m. Workout and shower would take me to, roughly, 11.30 a.m. whereupon I would meander up the Perth Road to arrive in plenty of time for the noon Pure Mathematics lecture. Finishing there at 1 p.m., I'd take another leisurely stroll back down to the Union, or into town, for a sandwich and a drink then head over to the Tower Building for the 2 p.m. Economics lecture. Then a 3 p.m. finish, the 3.15 p.m. TayWay bus to Carnoustie and back home just after 4 p.m. – it's a hard life! Sometimes there were changes to this schedule, but this rather leisurely regime was as enjoyable then as it sounds now.

One downer from that period, however, came in December 1980, while standing in the cold and dark at 8.30 a.m. waiting for the uni exam hall to open for our term Mathematics exam. Having totally got my head together as far as studying and doing what I needed to do, I was calm and focused, and actually looking forward confidently to the exam, when Neil wandered around the corner looking even more morose than he normally looked first thing in the morning.

"John Lennon's dead," were his first words, followed by, "Somebody shot him."

It was immediately obvious that he was serious, and not winding anyone up, and the mood that descended upon our little queue instantly matched that of the morning – cold and dark. It was a quite surreal moment and not something that was easily forgotten as we shuffled into the hall to take the exam. I don't remember anything about the exam itself, other than that I somehow must've cleared my head enough to get through it successfully. Afterwards I think we all just headed home without much further discussion, no doubt to wait for whatever news reports we could find on radio or TV – no 24-hour rolling news coverage in 1980 – and come to terms with what was, for our generation, a genuinely life-changing event.

But by far the most important thing that happened in my life around this time however was meeting the girl who was, literally, to change my life. By the time I got around to asking her out, in April 1981, she had already been on my radar for some considerable time – you know what I'm like by now!

At the start of the summer holidays in 1980 my brother, Tommy, and I decided to go to a Scottish FA coaching course being held at the College of Education playing fields. This was a great experience, held over two weekends.

Apart from learning about coaching it was great just to be playing football with professional players and coaches.

One of the coaches, Archie Knox, was player-manager of Forfar Athletic and he invited me to go to their pre-season training. That was absolutely fantastic.

On the first night, we ran all the way round Forfar Loch, stopping every so often to do strength circuits and sprints. Then we moved on to football drills and small-sided games before finishing off with timed 300 m sprints. I hadn't realised that people, even professional footballers, could run this far or this much! It was exhausting but absolutely exhilarating and I was in my element.

One funny thing that happened that first night was that, while we were playing the small-sided games, Archie sent his coach, Kenny, to lay out the cones for the sprinting session. When he called time on the games, we moved over to this running course that Kenny had set out in a curve. Archie looked at him and barked, "Why have you set it out like that? What was wrong with a straight line?"

There's a huge area of land around Forfar Loch and more than plenty of room for what Archie wanted.

Kenny replied, a little sheepishly it must be said, "Oh, sorry, boss, I didn't think. I always put the cones out in a curve when we're training back at the ground."

Archie went ballistic! "For f★★★'s sake, Kenny, that's an enclosed space!"

All of the players were falling about laughing, even me – although it was my first night I'd already been accepted as one of the lads – though maybe I was a bit more restrained than the regulars.

The training stepped up over the next few weeks and I was to discover what really being fit meant. I was also working, as usual, for the council during the day, so the combination of physical labour plus intensive training meant one very fit, very tired, very happy wee boy.

After about four weeks of training we played our first pre-season game, against Dundee. As a dyed-in-the-wool United supporter, this was a great opportunity for me and only added extra motivation. I played well, though it was to be my last involvement as I was heading off the next week to Stirling University for the next phase of my coaching education.

The B Licence course was a week-long residential and I was excited and apprehensive about it all in equal measure. I shouldn't have worried though – with the fitness I'd gained over the previous month, I was absolutely flying at the course.

During one of the practice matches I overheard Andy Roxburgh, then the Head of Coaching at the SFA, comment to a colleague "that boy's a player" after one of my contributions.

If the playing was going well, the coaching was disappointing as I was criticised for being "too quiet" and "lacking experience". I was advised to get more practical experience before returning for reassessment sometime in the future. Archie told me that I could come back to Forfar after the first month or so of the season had passed as he only wanted to work with his signed players at the start of the season, so everything was looking promising there. So, to fill in time before my big break I went back to playing for the university team at the start of my final year.

For the first few weeks this seemed pretty good. I had established myself within the group and seemed to be highly rated by the coach, Kenny Cameron, who knew me from the SFA courses. This all turned a little sour by the start of October, however.

For those first few weeks, the squad had consisted of the local boys and others who had chosen to stay on in Dundee during the summer break. As the new term approached, all the others returned and it very quickly became apparent that there was a definite clique and pecking order, and I wasn't part of it. Kenny, disappointingly, went along with this and I found myself selected for the second XI and apparently *persona non grata* with the regular first team.

No matter, I'll work my way back, I thought, naïvely.

I was also still awaiting the call to return to Forfar, but this was dealt a blow when Archie left to become co-manager at Aberdeen. His replacement, Alex Rae, also wanted me to return but wanted to settle in himself first.

Anyway, after a few weeks my frustration was starting to eat away at me and during one game with the uni team I disgraced myself by getting sent off for the one and only time in my career. And Dad was watching! Oh the shame. Seriously.

Actually, I still think it was undeserved. The referee, who was inept, had wrongly, in my humble but totally correct opinion, blew me up for offside as I broke through on goal. I admit, I flipped a little, and argued the point too loudly for too long, so he booked me. As I walked away from the caution I muttered, "I hope you pass your exams, ref."

He didn't take my good wishes in the spirit in which they were intended, or perhaps he did, as he promptly sent me off. Talk about a trumped-up charge though – when I received his official report of the incident he had me down as uttering the f-word virtually every second word. I hadn't sworn; I knew I hadn't, so I resolved to challenge this at the disciplinary hearing. This led to a salutary lesson on the futility of challenging petty authority without backup evidence. I was suspended for three or four games, can't remember exactly, and left to nurse my anger over the next few weeks.

When I returned, on my first or second game back, I injured my knee in a tackle and my friend Ricky drove me to the hospital A&E department. After sitting in a cubicle for about two hours, a doctor decided I had strained ligaments and only needed a Tubigrip. Another hour passed before a nurse came in carrying a basin and soap and said, "Can you wash your own leg? We're a bit short staffed!" The NHS, eh?

Another month and I was ready to return, but my enthusiasm was waning fast. First, the injury had cost me my chance at Forfar as the opportunity had now drifted away, and second, the standard of play in that second XI was dire. A few games into my return we were being well beaten 5–0 and the attitude of the guys was generally appalling. One or two of us were trying our guts out to get back into the game, but the rest had chucked it and seemed to think it was funny.

That did it for me and I left after that game, never to return. One or two of the good guys tried to talk me round, but that stubborn streak had kicked in again and I wasn't for changing.

"OK, but what's all this got to do with the girl who would change your life?" I hear you ask. Well, my football-dictated routine on a Saturday afternoon was to meander down to Carnoustie's main street to catch the bus to Dundee and, on the way, I would pop in to The Pepperbox to buy chewing gum. The Pepperbox was a Carnoustie institution, a confectionery, tobacconist and ice-cream shop with a wee café at the back. The owner was the irrepressible Dixie Marshall who employed various members of her family in addition to a steadily changing cast of young schoolgirls. Dixie had known me and my family for years and was always joking with my mum about this girl or that girl fancying her son. Anyway, none of those identified had ever interested me and I found it all a bit embarrassing really.

During this spell though, I had become aware of this gorgeous wee red-haired girl with beautiful eyes and a smile that lit up the shop. You know what it's like when you actually like someone, at that age anyway? The last thing you want to do is show it in any way, so everything becomes a bit awkward and shy, sideways glances and stilted conversation and all that. And so it went on.

I was devastated when I went into the shop around the New Year as she wished the guy in front of me, "Happy New Year," and gave him a kiss, while I only got the greeting. Later, she would confess that she remembered that incident, and that I didn't get the kiss because she liked me too! How exactly does the human race survive?

One of my other regular excuses for going in was when I would pick up *The Sporting Post* in the shop next door early on a Saturday evening and nip into The Pepperbox for, well, anything really, but principally to see if she was there and maybe, just maybe…

Anyway, on one of these visits I was greeted by the sight of her splendid rear end as she was upside down in a freezer cabinet, raking something out of the bottom. Unable to contain myself, I slapped it gently with my copy of *The Sporting Post* and receiving an "oy" and a massive smile as my reward for this exceptionally forward act. Maybe around then I was beginning to think that she might like me too, but I still didn't know her name. Yeah, yeah, why didn't I just ask? Why indeed!

Anyway, fate was to intervene as I chanced upon a photograph in *The Courier* one day of my mysterious obsession and finally had a name to put to her gorgeous face – Angela. It was a start! With the kind of low-level stalking that could get you arrested nowadays, this information was enough to find out where she lived via the phone book. Hence, I was able to hatch a plan to "accidentally" bump into her as she walked home from work one Saturday evening. This worked a treat and we chatted all nervous and giggly over the course of around 50 metres until, curses, a car drew up and some of her schoolfriends interrupted our flow. She went off with them and I carried on home, elated to have finally spoken properly to her and deflated that it had been abruptly terminated.

We continued skirting and flirting around each other for a wee while longer but by Eastertime I had decided that something had to give. I remember I was painting the outside of our house, the roans I think, and listening to the radio. "Angie" by the Rolling Stones came on and I took that as a sign that now was the time.

Just as I'd done all those years ago, I had a few false starts of walking past the phone box but eventually steeled myself and made the call.

Her mum answered. Rats! History was repeating itself.

Coolly I asked, "Is Angela in?"

And she just said, "Yes… It's for you, Angie," and handed the phone over.

Once again I was amazed at how easy it all seemed and we arranged to go to the cinema the next week. Why had I been putting this off? Would I ever learn?

The big day came and I set off to meet her at the end of her street to catch the bus to Dundee. I learned later that she understood nothing of my warblings on the bus because of the background noise but hadn't wanted to say so in case I thought there was something wrong with her, but she seemed to smile and laugh in all the right places so I thought it was all going well. It was probably just as well she couldn't hear me properly, mind, as I was so nervous I would definitely have been talking rubbish!

We headed for the Union, and when asked what she would like to drink she confidently replied, "Vodka, lime and soda please." Apparently when I then ordered a pint… of orange juice… for myself, she was panicking inside wondering if I'd think she was a drunk!

Anyway, drinks finished we made off for the cinema, the ABC, and saw the film *The Outsiders*. I'm convinced that's what it was at any rate – Angela hasn't got a clue!

On our next date, a few days later, we just went for a long walk around Carnoustie after she finished work. We were already, absolutely, an item and thoroughly besotted with each other. So much so that my announcement that I would be away at the weekend on a coaching course was not the best of news for either of us. Again, I later learned that Angela had thought we were cursed, having waited so long to get together then being apart for a whole weekend just as we were getting going. The welcome I received when I went round to her house the night I returned simply cemented our relationship and we were rarely out of each other's company thereafter – what a summer.

So, coaching course you say? Yes, although I'd been advised to "get more experience", I booked myself into the first available reassessment session. This time it was at Largs, the SFA coaching headquarters, and although everything went exceptionally well, the end result was the same. "Get more experience."

I was already getting fed up of this. I knew for a fact that I'd performed well enough, and certainly better than a couple of PE students who did pass. I was beginning to understand that this coaching ladder was not placed on an entirely level playing field. How's that for effortlessly mixing metaphors? Anyway, what with this experience and falling out with the uni football guys, football was about to take a wee bit of a back seat for a while, though I didn't quite realise it at this stage.

Despite being all loved up, I had the small matter of my final exams to attend to. I had, finally, learned the theory, practice and wisdom of studying and, with extra motivation provided by my new girlfriend, I got stuck into the most intensive period of revision and exam preparation that I had ever undertaken. The upshot was that I breezed confidently through the exams and had very little doubt in my mind that I had been entirely successful.

No matter how confident you are though there's always a nagging doubt at the back of your mind, so when the results were finally and officially announced it was a great relief. The graduation ceremony was to be on 26 June at the Caird Hall and all graduands were entitled to two tickets. Two tickets? I needed at least… one, two, three, four, five, six, seven, eight… eight! Thankfully, the wonderful Charlie Dixon came to my rescue and secured the additional tickets for me so that my proud day could be shared with Mum, Dad, Angela, Tommy, Pat and Gail, and Mum's two sisters, Nan and Bette. Three-piece navy-blue pinstripe suit specially purchased for the occasion, and I was good to go. I had to get a haircut before the graduation though... except, I never quite got around to that.

Funny how perceptions change though. My parents used to harp on at me to get my hair cut and were really annoyed that I hadn't got it cut for this occasion. Yet, in future years, Mum would point to my graduation photo and say, "Your hair was better like that," without any shred of embarrassment about how hard a time she'd given me for not getting it cut.

We joke about that picture now as representing my Cliff Richard phase as my hair looks very precise and glossy, even if it was too long for Ma and Pa at the time! It also reminds me of my dad's belated follow-up to his quackers joke from all those years ago – when he heard that I was now entitled to put BSc after my name, his immediate response was, "What does that stand for – brush, shovel and cartie?" Aye, another one that hasnae improved with age!

I had to get a day off work for the graduation and I spent the day before, indeed several weeks before, picking stones off a reclaimed section of Pitskelly Park in Carnoustie. It was a long, hot summer and being in the middle of a dustbowl all day was a nightmare for a peely-wally pale-skinned creature like me. I was astute enough to get sunscreen on... after I was burned, obviously... but its main quality was to provide an adhesive base for all of the grit and stour flying around as we picked up the stones! This added to the sunscreen properties, however, providing a physical barrier to augment the chemical barrier, and should maybe be considered by the pharmaceutical giants.

I remember coming home the day before the graduation and thinking that I would be sporting a fine suntan at the ceremony. One bath later and I was disavowed of that notion, as my suntan drained away down the plughole and my white-with-tinges-of-pink reflection stared back from the mirror.

The rest of the summer consisted of work, home, shower, change, eat… and meet Angela, a pattern no doubt familiar to all young lovers, then and now. We didn't do much in particular, just generally hung out in her house, my house or wandered round Carnoustie, but it was an idyllic summer.

We also had the public holiday afforded by the royal wedding of Charles and Diana. As a confirmed republican, this meant absolutely nothing to me but a day off's a day off, and a gloriously sunny day it was too. We went for a walk in the morning, returning to Angela's house in time to watch the wedding, me grudgingly, her enthusiastically.

Completely unrelated to the events of the day, that evening I asked her to marry me. What? Where did that come from? Yep, you read that right – I asked her to marry me. And she said, "Yes… but not now."

Timing is everything and mine was completely askew. She was due to head off to uni in Edinburgh, so marriage was out of the question. I think I knew that – I just wanted to demonstrate how completely head over heels I was and that was the only way I could think of. Anyway, she said "yes" and the rest was mere detail. Good things come to those who wait…

Sometime after the graduation I really did need a haircut, and Angela volunteered to do it. Trustingly, I let her loose and the result seemed OK. Until a few months later when I thought I'd better get it cut again before starting college.

"Who cut your hair last time?" enquired the hairdresser.

"My girlfriend," I replied, "why?"

"She's not a hairdresser, is she?"

"No."

"Thought not! Well, your hair's going to be a lot shorter than you thought it would be to rectify this mess!"

Hmm. Another lesson learned – never again.

October arrived and we were off into the unknown once again. Angela was away to Edinburgh, and I was starting at Dundee College of Education to do my one-year teacher training course. Her leaving was obviously very emotional, but it was an exciting time for her no matter how bad I felt about her leaving.

I didn't handle it well. I missed her constantly. I phoned her every night, no mean feat in the days before mobile phones, and I visited most weekends. This was quite an adventure, heading straight from college to the railway station on a Friday, arriving in Edinburgh sometime after 5 p.m. then walking up to Pollock Halls and a cuddlesome reunion around 6 p.m.

We had some great adventures around this time, exploring new restaurants and places and generally growing up, I suppose. Although I was chronologically 22 years old by now, I was a young 22. Not in any bad way, just naïve, inexperienced, shy, reserved and not at all worldly. I wasn't enjoying college, once again for a variety of reasons, but the weekends were a great escape and I was milking them to the extreme.

Why wasn't I enjoying it? Well the main reason would have to be that the naïve, inexperienced, shy, reserved and not at all worldly Gordie was completely and utterly lovesick!

The weekends were fantastic, and we experienced many things through in Edinburgh, but for every high there's an accompanying low, and for every excited Friday evening arrival there was a corresponding depths of despair return train journey late on Sunday evening.

Apart from all that, I just didn't take to the courses – everything just seemed so dry and stuffy, and it was hard to take one of our main lecturers seriously as he continually stuttered his way through sentences, saying "actually in fact" umpteen times as some kind of verbal tic – he'll make a somewhat ironic reappearance in a few paragraphs' time!

Not many of the psychology and educational theory classes seemed entirely relevant to what I recognised as teaching, though I would reverse that judgement a wee bit in hindsight, and some of the other classes were just bizarre. Principal amongst those was AVA or, to give it its full title, Aural and Visual Aids. That lost me on week one when the lecturer demonstrated the "correct" way to clean a blackboard, and he didn't redeem himself the following week when we were forced to construct signage using Letraset!

Once it became clear that the rest of the year would be spent carrying out similarly mundane practical projects, I hatched a cunning plan. I can't remember which day that class was on, but as it was first thing in the morning, my routine was to go into the base room and sign the register then turn around and head straight back out of the building, ensuring that I was on a bus to Carnoustie approximately half an hour after having been dropped off at the front door by my brother!

To achieve a pass, we were required to submit three pieces of practical work to demonstrate our AVA prowess, which I duly did by producing one photocopy (really), one Banda-copied worksheet and an OHP slide – I know, genius, eh? It still makes me laugh today that that course could ever have been offered to graduates about to enter the teaching profession.

The other class that sticks in my mind, for entirely different reasons, was in first aid. It was interesting enough, and learning the basics of things like recovery positions and resuscitation are obviously very important skills to have, but I remember it most for the day when one of our classmates, Ann, fainted for real and had to be carted off to see the college nurse! Ann was nice, and I think she had a thing for me – she even turned up in Edinburgh one time when I was visiting Angela, I think she was checking out the competition!

Rewinding a little, before actually starting at college, we had to arrange a few days of observation at a school of our choosing. I, naturally, chose Carnoustie High. And so we had the ridiculous juxtaposition of the long-haired guy who was cutting the grass at the school topless on the Friday afternoon turning up suited and booted on the Monday morning. Honestly, it couldn't have been scripted better! It certainly provided a couple of double takes from the pupils.

"Wasn't he… no, couldn't have been."

Yes, he was!

We then had two weeks at college to be followed by four weeks on placement then two weeks back for exams. My placement was… Carnoustie. As a student teacher you are basically allocated a full timetable – you just shadow the class teacher. The idea is that they let you take the occasional lesson and gradually give you more responsibility. I particularly thrived on being Ed's apprentice, and he gave me more responsibility quicker than most. Being a wily old fox, this may have been partly to afford himself respite from what wasn't the easiest class in the world, but I think it was more genuine than that as he was always there when I needed him.

In Term 2 we were to be out for six weeks and in college for four, and my six weeks were spent at Monifieth High. This was purely pragmatic, as it was the next closest to home. Same pattern, though one teacher took advantage – when I told him one day that I hadn't quite finished the topic I'd been allocated responsibility for he said dismissively, "Don't worry, if it had been important I'd have never let you do it anyway." Cheek!

One funny memory from that placement occurred after a crit lesson, so-called because that's when your college lecturer critiques your performance and the result counts towards your final grade. Anyway, for this lesson I was taking this second-year class and everything went entirely to plan, I delivered my lesson perfectly and the kids responded well and, importantly, behaved well too.

Afterwards, my lecturer gave me his feedback – "Well done, that all went well, but you must think about how you speak to the pupils – your accent is far too guttural," said the English guy with a stutter who'd never actually taught in a Scottish state school!

When I related this to the class teacher, who was also English, she told me to forget that ridiculous nonsense, and that she envied the rapport I had with her class because they related to my accent in a way that they never could to hers. What's that saying again? "You can't please all of the people all of the time."

Term 3 saw me at an inner-city school to break me out of the cosy suburbia offered by both Carnoustie and Monifieth – Menzieshill High in Dundee, chosen purely because I could visit my gran at lunchtime, was next up. I got a lift from a Biology teacher who insisted on leaving Carnoustie at 7.45 a.m. to be in school for 8.15 a.m. despite the fact nothing happened until 9 a.m. This was a very boring period! The kids were totally different too, a wee bit of a culture shock for me.

I remember taking one group of boys out to the playing fields to do a lesson on scale drawing. When I asked them to estimate the distance from the building to the fence, one of them said, "Estimate? We're Foundation ye ken."

"Take a guess," I clarified, to which he replied, "How'd ye no say that then?"

Another time, during a crit lesson, one girl loudly said to me, "Mr Craigie, is that mannie testing you?"

"Yes, he is," I replied.

"Hope he's daein it right cos you're good," she offered helpfully!

The Mathematics Department was totally dysfunctional, in my humble but inexperienced opinion at the time, with not much evidence of camaraderie among the teachers. One old guy wore a kilt, every day, completely oblivious to the incessant ridicule of the pupils. In a way I admired him as I was, and probably still am, way too self-conscious to have taken an extreme approach to what I was wearing.

During this final term, we were also obliged to apply for our first jobs. This was done regionally and, although I only wanted to work at Carnoustie High, this meant applying for Angus and Dundee as well in order to cover all the bases. When the interview for Angus came up I answered every question in the context of working at Carnoustie, and the Director of Education kept batting that away while reminding me that this was a general interview.

They gave the game away though when his advisor, a great old guy called Tim Morrison, finished with, "So, if Willie Simmons wants you to take a football team you'd be up for that then?" Clearly I was destined for Carnoustie!

So, although I felt confident of the right result, I still had to go through with the Dundee interview and they appeared very keen to have me back at Menzieshill. I learned many years later that the folks at Menzieshill had considered it a done deal and were surprised when I didn't turn up.

Anyway, without too much agonising the formal offer of employment at Carnoustie High School came in and was duly accepted.

Despite all of this job-related activity there was still the small matter of formally graduating from the college and this duly arrived without complication. Or so I thought. Again, many years later, I heard that someone in the college wanted to veto my graduating on the grounds of inadequate attendance – probably the AVA guy! – but that this had been quashed by Jim Lacey who had forcefully insisted, "I want him in my school." I'll say it again, it's always nice to be wanted!

So, the old navy-blue, three-piece pinstripe made another appearance and the much smaller college graduation ceremony was witnessed by Mum, Dad and Angela, and then, that was that. Student days over, back to a final grass-cutting stint and a summer of relative freedom.

The two standout memories from that summer of '82 touched both extremes of the happiness spectrum. Watching the legend that is David Narey score a wonderful opening goal for Scotland against Brazil in the World Cup – before the Brazilians woke up and retaliated with four of their own!

– remains the principal contender at the good end. At the other extreme, a trip to the Rollerama…

Angela decided that this would be an entertaining night out, but never having skated on either wheels or ice before, I think I was probably a wee bit reluctant, but whatever, nothing ventured and all that. She'd recently passed her driving test, so borrowed her dad's car and transported us to the recently opened Rollerama Indoor Skating Rink in Dundee.

As I took my first faltering steps onto the surface it was clear that my Bambi-on-ice technique was never going to get me anywhere, so Angela kindly offered coaching advice and linked arms with me in an attempt to guide me around. This went well for probably all of about 30 seconds until my legs and arms started flailing wildly in a vain attempt to stay upright. Despite Angela's best efforts to stabilise me, we both went crashing to the floor, much to our mutual embarrassment. If only that was the end of it…

Angela was in agony, and her left wrist wasn't pointing in the same direction that it had been moments earlier. This was scary for both of us, but obviously much more worrying for her, so we quickly ditched the rollerblades and retrieved our shoes and drove up to the A&E department at the nearby Royal Infirmary – I drove, obviously.

Our worst fears were realised when the X-ray confirmed a break and her wrist was put in a plaster cast. I then drove us back to Carnoustie and when we arrived at her parents' house, much earlier than expected, and delivered the news, it was her dad's reaction that was the most memorable: "Who drove the car?" I'm sure he was worried about his daughter's well-being too but, ever the pragmatist, he wanted to make sure his car was OK!

Apart from the obvious pain and inconvenience of the whole incident it also meant that Angela returned to Edinburgh University a few weeks later with her left arm still encased in a stookie – maybe this is the time to introduce the fact that she's left-handed? So, not an ideal start to her second year of studies but she just got on with things, as she always does. She has, however, never let me forget that I broke her wrist all those years ago. Harsh!

And then, all too soon, the summer had ended and with it, the innocence of studying and of young Gordon having no discernible responsibilities. The world of work awaited...

EPILOGUE

Paperback writer

(2020)

Dear Sir or Madam
Will you read my book?
It took me years to write
Will you take a look?

It's confession time – this book was originally conceived, and the first draft written, in the spring of 2012, but is only being completed now, the summer of 2020 – I did mention more than once during the book that there's no point in rushing these things!

Why has it taken so long? Well, writing the first draft was cathartic, as it was written in the aftermath of life-changing events for both myself and my wife, Angela – you know, the wee girl that was introduced in the last chapter?

We both lost our fathers in 2011, within weeks of each other, and, having both lost our mothers some years previously, we were then essentially orphaned. It was a traumatic time for us both. So, for me, the act of actively remembering times that my family had shared in, even if many of them were vicarious, was helpful. It was also good to live inside my younger head for a wee while, and visualise the many happy times growing up and the adventures of changing from a wee boy to a young man.

Yet, having done all of that reflection, I was loath to go back and finish it off. Why? Well Angela would probably say indolence, but I would simplistically put it down to my expert-level tendency to procrastinate – finishing it off would involve making decisions, and we've already seen that those generally don't bring out the best in me! But, seriously, for whatever reason, it just never felt like the right time to finish it off, and it does now.

So, to answer the question posed in the prologue, is the book an autobiography or a memoir? Well, it's turned out to be about recollections, about emotions, about people and places, and though it is organised pretty much chronologically I think it would more accurately be described as a memoir, so that's what it is then! It attempts to answer the question *How Did I Get Here?* by placing these recollections largely on a timeline and allowing me to contextualise and understand from a distance. Yes, it's all rear-view mirror stuff, but for the first time I've also viewed it all through a wide-angled lens. And, dear reader, I've invited you to join me in the journey. But only so far on the journey as, if you've been paying attention, the last chapter finishes with me about to enter genuine adulthood, leaving full-time education behind and embracing the responsibilities of earning a living as a professional, as a teacher.

So there's more to come, another book's worth in fact, that'll pick up where this one leaves off and probably also include some things that I've forgotten from this one, maybe presented as some kind of dream sequence? So there's some good news for you if you've enjoyed the story so far, though probably completely irrelevant if you haven't!

But why would you join me? Like I said before, I'm not a celebrity and I'm not, and have no desire to be, famous, so why would you read this? For precisely those reasons! This is about me, clearly, but it's also about you, about all of us, who are not living our lives in the public eye.

Going back to that fateful freezing-cold run, when I first thought of an outline and a rationale for the book, I did wonder if it was just for me and mine, and maybe it is? But I remembered two autobiographies that I'd read around that time and instinctively felt that my tale stood up well to them.

Although he's very famous now, Chris Evans relates his early life as an ordinary guy in *Memoirs of a Fruitcake* particularly well. OK, part of the attraction to the book is that he is now famous and that large parts of the book focus on his drive to become famous, but the really interesting bits, for me, are about the extraordinary ordinariness of his early recollections and of the people, places and events outwith his celebrity bubble once he'd made it.

The other one that resonated with me was by a guy called Stephen Foster. Even while I was reading *From Working-Class Hero to Absolute Disgrace* I didn't know he had any profile at all. He is, apparently, a successful author, but I'd never heard of him and he most certainly does not live a celebrity life. So the book stood on the merits of his tale, and the fact that readers, myself included, presumably identified with his experiences.

I didn't even necessarily think it was particularly well written – sorry, Stephen – but the narrative kept me interested and I suppose that's my point. Hopefully you will think my effort is well written and also holds your interest!

And now, in 2020, in the midst of a global pandemic, I've just finished Pete Paphides' autobiography, *Broken Greek*, and again, although Pete is relatively famous and well connected, his story doesn't trade on his adult achievements but instead relates an absorbing tale of a shy young boy finding his way to adulthood in his own way – I'd like to think that accurately describes this volume too.

I have, intentionally, not revealed any salacious details, if indeed any exist, and I have not, I hope, revealed anything to embarrass anyone, not least myself. I've also not taken the opportunity to settle scores by identifying too many people who may have wronged me, as to do so would only inflate their importance in my development way beyond whatever it actually was. As my dad used to say, "whit disnae kill ye maks ye stronger", and I hope, and believe, that I've emerged stronger from any of the relatively few bad experiences I may have encountered.

So now that you've waded through both a prologue and epilogue, and all ten chapters in between, I hope you've enjoyed it. Maybe it'll inspire you to have your very own *How Did I Get Here?* moment and, if it does, I hope you find the experience as rewarding as I have. And please, come back again for the rest of the story...